THE EAST-WEST DICHOTOMY

The Conceptual Contrast Between
Eastern and Western
Cultures

Thorsten J. Pattberg

© 2009 Thorsten J. Pattberg

All rights reserved

ISBN-10 : 0984209107

ISBN-13 : 978-0984209101

Preface

The 'East-West dichotomy' is a philosophical concept of ancient origin which claims that the two cultural hemispheres, East and West, developed diametrically opposed, one from the particular to the universal and the other from the universal to the particular; the East is *more* inductive while the West is *more* deductive. Together they form an *equilibrium*...

Contents

History

Induction and Deduction

The Dichotomy with Asiacentrism

Equilibrium

Demography

Migration

Cultural Effects of the Dichotomy

Two Successful Models

Two Incommensurable Realities

The Theory of Power and to Whom It Belongs

The Problem of Standard

A Loveless Darwinian Desert

The Psychology of Communion

Cultural Evolution

A Copernican Revolution

The Problem with Nature

Truths and Values

Ideology

Gender

The Dialectics of Dichotomy

Problems with the Dichotomy

The Future of the Dichotomy

The Author

References

East is East, and West is West,
and never the two shall meet.

Rudyard Kipling (1895)

A dichotomy – is any splitting of a whole
into exactly two non-overlapping parts.
Nothing can belong simultaneously to both parts.

Wikipedia (2008)

History

Herodotus (484 BC-425 BC), the 'father of history' (*Cambridge Dictionary*, 1999), was possibly the first recorded historian who deliberately portrayed the 'East' (Persians) and the 'West' (Greeks) as mutual antagonists, thereby proposing the nucleus of all ancient history. Others, Thucydides (460 BC-400 BC), and Xenophone (430 BC-354 BC), similarly, found it natural to employ strong polarities and concentrate on the 'otherness' of the East, while accepting the necessity of resistance to external force by defining a Western 'self.' Thus came into being the first system of the so-called East-West dichotomy.

In another part of the world, meanwhile, the ideas of Confucian China (551 BC-479 BC) and unification prevailed in the feudal states of the Eastern Zhou period (starting in 770 BC), spurred by the constant menace of invasion by exterior barbarians.

Meanwhile, the Aryan masters of the Indus Valley who had long merged with the Dravidian inhabitants started to unite their tribes and founded kingdoms (1500 BC-400 BC), and as a matter of survival against aggressors from the West created their own classical Indian culture and identity in opposition to the categorical otherness of the West.

As I see it, there have been only two configurations of the East-West dichotomy throughout history. The first one was Western-centered (Eurocentric, c. 500 BC-1950), the second one is Eastern-centered (Asiacentric, c. 1950-present). The former can be divided into Hellenic-Greek (c. 500 BC-0), Judeo-Christian (c. from the birth of Jesus Christ to AD 1500) and North-Atlantic (c. 1500-1950); the latter one exclusively relies on the growing influence of China and its periphery (c. 1950-present) alone. To my knowledge, no other 'centrism' has ever prevailed in world affairs. It is said in some academic circles that there has been a time when China was believed to be the supreme civilization, with all her great inventions like paper (220 BC), gunpowder (900), printing (1040), and the compass (1100) (Needham, 1964). Yet, to my understanding and despite those obvious accomplishments, China's contributions to the external world, her encounter with and influence on the Western hemisphere have been scarce and almost insignificant. Some have argued that the "invention of the sciences" was the single decisive advantage that put the West ahead of all the other civilizations. We should have serious doubts about this. Thousands of Greeks marched into Persia to aid Cyrus (c. 400 BC); the conquest of Alexander the Great (356 BC-323 BC), the Romans and their emperors (27 BC-AD 395), the crusades (eleventh-fifteenth centuries), the explorations and conquests by the Mediterranean world (fifteenth-sixteenth centuries), the missionaries (sixteenth-seventeenth centuries), the colonial powers (sixteenth-nineteenth centuries), the subjugation of the New World (fifteenth-sixteenth centuries), the invention of the sciences (seventeenth century), and now globalization – all are products of the West. In a distinct succession, the West had always descended upon the 'others' before they did the same: The envy of the world was the Greeks, the tormentor of the world was Christianity, and the leader of the world was

Europe/America, more or less indisputably so until the second half of the twentieth century.

I would like to argue then, that with the shattering of Europe during the two world wars (1914-18 and 1938-45), the collapse of the colonial empires, the rise and (later) fall of the Soviets, and with China's first experiments with Western 'narratives' (e. g. Marxism/Communism), Asian dominance had silently set in the second half of the twentieth century. History speaks for itself: In the following 50 years, according to the United Nations (UN), there were 118 wars (compared to just 55 in the first half of the century), not surprisingly most of them driven or fueled by anti-Western sentiments, most notably the Cold War (1950-1989). The USA, at least involved in 60 of these wars, was defeated in Korea (1950-1953, officially a UN operation), Vietnam (1965-1972), during the Suez-Crisis (1956, together with Britain and France), and, most recently, failed in Afghanistan (2002-2006) and Iraq (2004-2008, both with the UK and other nations). In the meantime, we have seen the rapid economic development of no less than nine Eastern 'tiger-states' or regions: Taiwan, Hong Kong, Singapore, South Korea, Indonesia, Malaysia, Thailand, Dubai and the Philippines.

Some people say that the two poles of the East-West dichotomy had shifted twice to the out-most peripheries of the world, in the East to Japan (c. 1868-1945) and in the West to the USA (c. 1950-2006). I have strong objections against this. Japan, despite her relative military and economic power, like Great Britain, is an island state with the historical function of manipulating power structures between the divided forces dwelling on the massive neighboring continent. However, being descendants of the great landmasses themselves (Germanic and Chinese/Korean), with relatively small populations, neither of them fits the East-West equation by itself. The USA, on the other hand, is not a civilization but a (Western) culture, living on the outer crescent of the world's pivot: Eurasia.

Halford Mackinder had suggested as early as 1904 that the natural seat of power of all existing civilizations (except Latin American civilization) – Western, Confucian, Japanese, Islamic, Hindu, Slavic-Orthodox, African, with a combined population of 5.6 billion (or 85 percent of the Earth's population) – is the continuous landmass of Eurasia and the subcontinent Africa, often referred to together as the 'World Island' (Mackinder, 1904). Let us say then that for the past 2,500 years, the history that mattered most was that of the European people, continuously reinventing themselves either through their struggle against Asiatic invasion (Persians, Ottomans, Arabs etc.), or through conquest and colonization, and consequently exercising their authority over all defining paradigms in any East-West dispute, be it on a philosophical, scientific, economic, or ideological level.

Now, as all theses tend to have antitheses, the balance for supremacy over the other civilizations is going to tip in favor of the ever more influential power blocks of Asia: China (with Taiwan, Hong Kong, South Korea, Indonesia, Malaysia, Vietnam etc.), Japan, and soon India. And, because of their different cultural outlooks and sets of beliefs and values, these Eastern peoples will inevitably redefine history and reevaluate the East-West dichotomy according to the needs and benefits of their own triumphant civilizations.

Naturally, it won't take long until they will try to dominate.

Induction and Deduction

西方文化注重分析，一分为二；
而东方文化注重综合，合二为一。
*The West is deductive, from the universal to the particular;
the East is inductive, from the particular to the universal.*
(Ji Xianlin, 2006 [1])

According to the universal historians Arnold Toynbee (1889-1975), Samuel Huntington (1927-), and Ji Xianlin (1911-2009), the world's states form 21, 23, or 25 spheres, nine civilizations, and fall into four cultural systems: Arabic/Islamic, Confucian, Hindi/Brahmin, and Western/Christian, with the former three forming the Oriental cultural system, and the latter one the Occidental cultural system (Toynbee, 1961; Huntington, 1993; Ji, 2006). The main difference between the Orient and the Occident, so people say, lies in their different modes of thinking: The East is inductive; the West is deductive.

Hence, the Orient's search for universal formulas describing balance, harmony, or equilibrium: For example, in Chinese philosophy, the two lines in Chinese 二 (er, two) mean weight and counterpoise. Similarly, we find 入入 (ru-ru, enter-enter) meaning equal weight on both sides, 巾 (liang, equilibrium) representing scales in equilibrium (Wieger, 1965), or 阴阳 (yin and yang) meaning two opposing but complementary primal forces. There are also Japanese ぜん (禅, zen) and 空 (śūnyata, emptiness) meaning everything is interrelated. In India we find seva-nagri (the universe and I are one and the same) and tat tvam asi (thou art that) meaning that the soul is part of the universal reality.

By means of continuously inducing the universal, Confucianism, Daoism, Shintoism, Hinduism, and Buddhism – as a rough guide – all ultimately arrive at the universal concept of 'the One,' 'oneness of heaven and man' (天人合一, tian ren he yi), the 'divine law' behind the *Vedas*, the 'merger of Brahman and atma' (Brahmatmaikyam) or 'ultimate reality'

(Ayam atma bhrama), the underlying inductive principle being that 'All observed things are connected, therefore all things are one.'

In inductive reasoning, one induces the universal 'all things are one' from the particular 'all things' that are 'observed.' The conclusion may be sound, but cannot be certain.

In the *Bodhicaryavatara*, a key text of Mahayana Buddhism, Santideva (c. 650) teaches us that the fate of the individual is linked to the fate of others (Williams, 1998):

> Hastadirbhadeva bahuprakarah yathaikah parinatyaniyah tatha jagad bhinnamabhinna duhkh-sukhanmakam sarvamidam tartheva.
> *Although our human body is made of various parts we do not feel them as separated. Likewise this world is made of various elements but it is inseparable – it is one.*
> (Santideva, 650).

In the *Abhidarma Sutra* (*The Higher Teachings of Buddha*) of the *Tipitaka* (c. 100 BC), Lord Buddha says there is no 'person,' 'individual,' or 'I' in reality – it is all one 'Ultimate Truth' (Tipitaka, 2008). Nagarjuna (c. 200), writer of the

Madhyamika-karika, adds: To attain Nirvana is to achieve 'absolute emptiness' (Bapat, 1956). For D. T. Suzuki (铃木 大拙, 1870-1966) 'Zen' is about the 'Ultimate Nothingness' (Suzuki, 1994). In Hinduism, the great epic *Mahabharata* (c. 600 BC-AD 400) reads: "Yad ihasti tad anyatra yan nehasti na tat kvachit" or "What is found here, can be found elsewhere. What is not found here will not be found elsewhere" (*Mahabharata,* 2009). In the *Bhagavadgita* (ca. 150 BC), Krishna says to Arjuna: "Mamaivamsho jiva-loke jiva-bhutah sanatanah" ("The living entities in this conditional world are my fragmental parts, and they are eternal") (*Bhagavadgita,* 2008).

In the *Book of Changes* (*I Ching*, 易经; c. 1050-256 BC) 'One' is the supreme ultimate. In the *Dao De Jing* (道德经, c. 600 BC), Lao Zi (老子) says "一生二，二生三，三生万物" ("One gives birth to two, two gives birth to three, three gives birth to all things") (Lao Zi, 42). Confucius, too, discovered the oneness of heaven (天, tian) and man (人, ren) and rejoiced: "五十而知天命" ("At fifty I understood the decrees of heaven"), and later: "天生德于予" ("Heaven produced that virtue in me") (Confucius, *Lun Yu,* 2;4, 7;23). We find similar notions in *The Book of Mencius*: "尽其心者，知其性也； 知其性则知天矣"

("If you fully explore your mind, you will know your nature. If you know your nature, you know heaven") (Mencius, 7A.1), Dong Zhongshu: "天人之际，合而为一" ("Heaven and men are a unit; they form the one") (Dong, 13; 56), and Lao Zi again: "人法也，地法天，天法道，道法自然" ("Man takes his law from the Earth; the Earth takes its law from Heaven; Heaven takes its law from the Dao. The law of the Dao is its being what it is") (Lao Zi, 25).

Note the implied universality: In the search for absolute interconnectedness, induction does not rely on categorical (formal) logic, hence the 'particular West,' by inductive inference, is included in this universal 'oneness,' or, as Nishitani Keiji (1900-1990) once nicely put it (Sueki, 2004): "Western modernity is to be overcome by the Eastern religious mind."

While the vigorous deductive West occupied foreign terrain, built churches, and spread the Gospel, the inductive East entertained a certain passivity, albeit with a long-term holistic world view:

We firmly believe, no matter how long it requires, the day will be with us when universal peace and the world of oneness will finally come true. (Ji Xianlin, 1996)

The West, on the other hand, separates God and the world. After all, we are not Him, but created by Him: "Then God said, Let us make man in our image; in the image of God he created him" (Genesis 1; 31).

Accordingly, in Western classrooms we teach an analytical 'concrete reality' based on conditioned textual analysis and interpretation of the world, rather than a holistic 'absolute reality.' Some examples of major works of analytical reasoning are Euclid's *Elements* (c. 300 BC), Kant's Copernican Revolution (1787), Darwin's theory of evolution (1859), Einstein's Logic of Continuity (1905), or Smith's *The Wealth of the Nations* (1776), the underlying deductive principle (as old as the Greeks themselves) being that: "All observed men are unique, Socrates is a man, therefore Socrates is unique."

In deductive reasoning, one deduces the particular 'Socrates is unique' from the universal 'all men are unique,' relying on the premises 'Socrates is a man' and 'All men are unique.' The conclusion is sound and valid.

A world thus described by deductive reasoning reaches new conclusions from previously known facts *ad infinitum*. A world by inductive reasoning, on the other hand, allocates relations to recurring phenomenal patterns. We may call the former a "string of cause and effect," whereas in the latter we see a "puzzle made of its parts."

Accordingly, in the same way as some cultures believe in one, many, or no gods at all, they also have different ways of perceiving the world and reasoning about it: Western civilization became *analysis-based*, while the Orient became *integration-based*.

I believe in this peculiar difference, and I suppose that most of those acquainted with Oriental thought do too. Yet I do not believe the West and the East are two mysterious forces bound for confrontation as in *The Clash of Civilizations* by Samuel P. Huntington (1993), nor do I believe that one is inevitably superior and the other necessarily inferior in accumulating either wealth or wisdom as in *The Protestant Ethic* by Max Weber (1930) or in *The Eastern Religious Mind* by Nishitani Keiji (1942). For my part, I believe there has been a difference in the independent development of the two great cultural systems, deeply embedded since their earliest histories, in symbiosis with their peoples, and arranged according to their cultural outlooks – *deduction* and *induction*.

In *La Route de la Soie* Aly Mazahéri quoted this ancient Persian and Arab saying from the Sassanian Dynasty (226-c. 640):

The Greeks never invented anything except some theories. They never taught any art. But the Chinese were different. They did teach all their arts, but indeed had no scientific theories whatever. (Ji Xianlin, 1996)

I will not go so far as Mazahéri to say "they do only this, and we do only that," nor will I claim that someone is definitely deductive in outlook just because he was born in London. It is not that easy. The making of every civilization's treasures and contributions to history is determined by its methodology for explaining the world's phenomena according to its own experience and mode of rational interpretation: The East became more inductive, while the West became more deductive – this appears to be borne out by all the evidence.

Let us next discuss how there has been an imbalance in the equilibrium and how Asiacentrism, after the first half of the twentieth century, has played a role in correcting this imbalance, and the history that led to it.

The Dichotomy with Asiacentrism

Man is the measure of all things.
(Protagoras, c. 480 BC-410 BC)

In the early twentieth century, the influences of such great (read: radical) narratives' doctrines such as Herbert Spencer's 'Social Darwinism' in "Process: Its Law and Cause" (1857), Friedrich Nietzsche's 'Will to Power' in *Human, All Too Human* (1886), and Karl Marx's *Communist Manifesto* (1848) could be felt in most Western academic writings on the East-West discourse. There was no sense of equilibrium and balance. In that great Darwinian struggle among nations for survival, any inferior culture was – at the slightest sign of weakness – believed to be surely eliminated. This gave rise to those misguided beliefs about superiority of race, culture, and civilization, for example in Nazi Germany (1933-1945) or militarist Japan (1932-1945), but also during Stalin's revolution (1928-32), the 1915-1917 massacres of Armenians under the Ottoman Empire, or Mao's Cultural Revolution (1966-1976). American cultural militarism (c. 1991-2006) is another case in point. Fortunately, another world war now seems unlikely. The world got a rude but timely awakening in August 1945, when an American bomber dropped a plutonium bomb, the so-called 'Fat Man,' over Nagasaki and ended World War II. Waging war on a grand scale, it seemed, stopped short at the prospect of total annihilation of entire civilizations. With Europe on her knees and the victorious USA well disposed to face the disciplined nations of the East (identified by the Warsaw Pact [1955-1991] and other communist nations), soon a new warfare had been created. This time, the warfare was merely ideological, if not intellectual:

According to the intrinsic powers of Western analytical reasoning over history, the East had to become gradually Westernized by law of nature.

Similar to the extension of the universe, demonstrable after the discovery of the 'Planck Constant' (Planck, 1901), or the direction of time, demonstrable by applying the 'Special Theory of Relativity' (Einstein, 1905), for the *analytically-based* West history has a *qualitative* nature. It has aim, it is progressive in nature, it can only improve in one direction, from a general (the universal) to a more complex stage (the particular), and advance with one truth only.

For the *integration-based* East, on the other hand, what might be called 'truth' is given at any time (the 'one') and is always justifiable through 'being a part of the whole.' In other words, there are many truths, many more than the West can bear, and the mere existence of the more inductive East as an alternative *a priori* to the more deductive West qualifies it to provide a genuine, believable non-Western experience of history: history as a non-directional but timeless tangible realm.

The integration-based East, for the greater part of its 5,000 years of extraordinary civilization (in the case of India and China, certainly even more), nurtured the importance of inductive reasoning by placing a strong emphasis on broadening all traditional knowledge, increasing its peoples' capacity for memorization, favoring the ability to learn from analogy, and promoting the skill to understand what is implied (for example, in Asia, 'yes' is the universal affirmative answer in formal dialog, even if 'no' is implied).

And then there is the Asian 'love of learning.' The subject of philosophical discussion as early as Mozi (墨子, 470 BC-391 BC), the love of learning was officially politicized during the Legalist Movement (770 BC-221 BC). The Legalists stressed the universal importance of promoting capable people as officials, regardless of their confession or creed. Throughout history, the inductive way in Asia manifested itself in an ever-increasing ability to reason inductively and, consequently, in cultural output (in art, religion, music, literature etc.) that values 'oneness,' 'balance,' and 'harmoniousness' (Gu, 1922; Sen, 2006; Wu, 1997, 1998). This overall output of Asian diligence, high achievement, and ancient commitment to study is best exemplified by Confucius' *Analects* (*Lun Yu*, 论语, 8;17):

学如不及，犹恐失之。
Study as if you were never to master it;
as if in fear of losing it.

So, that is essentially what the intelligent Asian people were doing in the twentieth century: studying as if they were never to master it. And, indeed, after prolonged flirtations with Western culture and values, especially during the 1911 Revolution and the May Fourth Movement (c. 1919-1921), which were essentially anti-Confucian and partly pro-Western, in the 1920's to 1930's virtually every Chinese, Japanese, or Indian intellectual was embroiled in a series of controversies about Eastern and Western culture (Ji, 2006).

Although Western theories, science, and technology were appreciated, most Eastern intellectuals were convinced that Asian values and wisdom were unique and so clearly diametrically opposed to many values and wisdom of the West, that they needed to be preserved, even at the cost of an inevitable intellectual clash with the West. In the fields of art, literature, and science, especially after the founding of the Communist Party in 1921, Chinese writers, politicians, and historians stood up for their views on the East-West dichotomy and patriotically defended their own civilization and the 'essence of the East' (e. g. Asian thought and culture) against the infiltration of Western "scum and dregs" as asserted by Ji Xianlin: "只要拿得不过头，不把西方文化的糟粕和垃圾一并拿来，就是好事" ("As long as we do not take in Western scum and dregs, it will be a good thing") (Ji, 2006 [2]), Western preoccupation with 'ontological beingness' as asserted by Kitaro Nishida 1870-1945 (Abe, 1988), and Western-fabricated 'Orientalism,' as Edward Said called it (Said, 1978; 1995).

Following the example of Japan's modernization efforts during the Meiji Restoration from the late ninteenth to the early twentieth century to absorb Western thought and technology ('Wakon yosai' or 'Western techniques, Japanese soul'), China and her neighbors, according to their 5,000 years of history of learning and self-cultivation reactively studied and Easternized virtually each and every Western theory. Hands down, I mean it: virtually everything.

Notwithstanding its love of learning, Confucian China, Imperial China, and now communist China nevertheless believed that the most important thing it already owned was 中国为本 (Chineseness at the root). If only she could acquire from the deductive, scientific-oriented USA and Europe their useful techniques and theories, the so-called *xifang wei mo* (西方为末, Westerness as a means)! In order to prevail over the West (Ji, 2006), do as the Master said:

三人行，必有我师焉；
择其善者而从之，其不善者而改之。

In strolling in the company of just two other persons, I am bound to find a teacher. Identifying their strengths, I follow them, and identifying their weaknesses, I reform myself accordingly. (Confucius, *Lun Yu*, 7,12).

Under 'Orientalization' we now understand the process in which Western knowledge and techniques are acquired without giving away the Asian soul – in essence a form of ideological self-reliance (自力更生), as opposed to reliance on Western ideology or Westernization.

Not only China, but East Asia in general consequently 'borrowed' from the West whatever seemed fit: from aestheticism in a Wildean or Byronic sense (Zhou, 2000), architecture, art and cinema, economics, film and documentary, law, literature, sports, music, post-modern theory, through Darwinism, Marxism (e.g. the Sinification of Marxism), to socialism (e.g. Socialism with Chinese characteristics) and new forms of democracy. The People's Republic of China today openly acknowledges the Democratic People's Republic of Korea, the Russia Federation, and Myanmar as 'democratic' nations and sees itself as 'democratic, with Chinese characteristics,' according to each country's own definition of what constitutes a legitimate democracy (China.org., 2005; Lynch, 2007). Remember the Eastern notions of many truths? That's a no-no in the Western world, where we expect the unwavering truth, and one truth only.

China in particular never made any great attempts at concealing her own truths and her aim to uphold Eastern values and wisdoms – why should the East throw away its five millennia of successful history and culture? – and at the same time profited from the practicability of foreign learning and her ability to adapt herself, even if it meant aggressively copying from the West:

师夷之长技以制夷。
Study the foreigners so that you will have the upper hand over them. (Wei Yuan, 1843)

All things Western became fashionable. However, the influence of Westerners on China's soil – as some patronizing American or European would like to imagine – as was truly the case with Buddhism in China (c. 68-800) or the introduction of Western sciences by European missionaries (c. 1575-1702) before, is wishful thinking. That 'Great Learning' from the end of the Qing Dynasty (清朝) onwards to the beginnings of the

People's Republic (1911-1949) is unmistakably 'made in China,' her 'intellectual property,' so to speak. I feel the urge to repeat this important historical fact: The rise of China is inherently Chinese, just as the Meiji Restoration (明治维新, Meiji Ishin, 1868-1912) was inherently Japanese.

Yes, Lu Xun (鲁迅, 1881-1936) adopted some ideas of Nietzsche's and developed them further. So did Li Shicen (李石岑, 1892-1934) and Mao Dun (矛盾, 1896-1981). Hu Shi (胡适, 1891-1962) espoused James's and Dewey's ideas on education and pragmatism and developed them further. Mao Zedong (毛泽东, 1893-1976), Chen Duxiu (陈独秀, 1879-1942), and Li Dazhao (李大钊, 1888-1927) were influenced by Marx and Lenin and developed their ideas further. I could go on. Yet no foreigner was involved in the intellectual output of those great cultural figures. The Chinese intellectuals – no less engaged in protecting their cultural sovereignty with nationalism than the Japanese before them – read Western theories, studied, improved, and Sinosized them.

In the integration-based East, where knowledge comes from tradition, ancient concepts of the inductive Eastern 'moral superiority' vs. Western deductive 'scientific superiority' were soon identified as the nucleus of the East-West dichotomy and the struggle for the 'Eastern soul.' By all means, Western technology and ways of rational inquiry, i.e. the deductive way, had to be acquired in order to defend against Western imperialism, yet it was the humanitarian Eastern soul and its wisdom, i.e. the inductive way, that should guide the East:

对西方的文化，鲁迅先生曾主张"拿来主义"。这个主义至今也没有过时。过去我们拿来，今天我们仍然拿来，只要拿得不过头，不把西方文化的糟粕和垃圾一井拿来，就是好事，就对我们国家的建设有利。

In the case of Western culture, Lu Xun earlier proposed the 'take-in approach.' This has ever since been our practice. In the past we took in, and today we are still taking in. As long as we steer calm, not taking in the waste and garbage of Western culture too, this will be a good thing for the construction of our nation.
(Ji Xianlin, 2006 [3])

Lu Xun proposed to "return a plum" (Ji, 2006). So does the Chinese tradition in the *Book of Songs*, Da Ya (诗经, 大雅): "投我一桃，报之以李" ("If you give me a peach, I shall return a plum"), meaning a give-and-take approach (送去主义). Unfortunately, Mao Zedong, realizing that the capitalist West would never accept his plum – with reference to Luo Guanzhong's (罗贯中) war epic *Romance of the Three Kingdoms* (三国演义, *San Guozhi*, c. 1330-1400) that reads: "三十年河西，三十年河东" ("Thirty years West of the river, thirty years East of it") (Luo, 1998) – mocked Lu Xun's give-and-take approach and disposed of tolerance altogether:

我认为现在国际形势到了一个新的转折点。世界上现在有两股风：东风，西风。中国有句话："不是东风压倒西风，就是西风压倒东风。我认为目前形势的特点是东风压倒西风，也就是说，社会主义的力量对于帝国主义的力量占了压倒的优势。

I believe that the international situation has now reached a new turning point. There are two winds in the world, the East Wind and the West Wind. There is a Chinese saying that "either the East Wind prevails over the West Wind or the West Wind prevails over the East Wind." I believe it is characteristic of the situation today that the East Wind is prevailing over the West Wind. That is to say, the forces of

Socialism have become overwhelmingly superior to the forces of Imperialism. (Mao Zedong, 1957)

In the latter half of the twentieth century, just as the West aggressively propagated its own political values, so did the East. The 'soul of Asia' had to be internalized by each and every member of its collective Eastern societies obedient to a universal Asiatic 'code of conduct' (e.g. Confucian conduct) driven by the Eastern notion of 'oneness.' Some may call it a collective defense mechanism against the Western 'particulars,' only this time using neo-Darwinian terminology in the spirit of Charles Darwin (and later Herbert Spencer) and their prophetic biology that "bids all to eat and to be eaten in their turn" (Darwin, 1859 [1]). If interest in biological survival embraces political resolutions, one may call it 'nationalism.'

Finally, the spiritual East identified the material West as its sole competitor for everything that is worthwhile in life: culture, values, wealth, and, yes, dignity. Yet, because of the limits of the inductive way, the East could only make sense of the West as a short-sighted, destructive force composed of millions of self-determined individuals who spread out and conquer nature, who undermine the 'great harmony,' thereby constantly neglecting the 'oneness of all things' and dwelling in the 'minuscule particular.' What was worse, back home the West had formed nation states as political tools to bundle and channel the disruptive forces of its armies of independent, egoistic, shameless, and often lonely individuals.

Not surprisingly, European-style nationalism and concepts of cultural superiority soon became very fashionable in the East, too, for example with eugenics in China. Until recently, the prevailing notion among many Chinese anthropologists, the Communist Party of China, and Chinese college textbooks well into the twenty-first century was that the Chinese race exclusively developed from the 'Peking Man,' or *homo erectus*, whose remains were, so we are told, first discovered in 1923 to 1928 by Davidson Black (1884-1934) and Pei Wenzhong (裴文中, 1904-1982) during excavations in Zhou Koudian (周口店), now a UNESCO World Heritage Center near Beijing that dates back roughly 500,000 years ago. Meanwhile, the European races were believed to be the result of interbreeding between *homo sapiens* and the lesser Neanderthal man. This interpretation of history was challenged twice in 1985 by Lewis Binford (1930-) and Chuan Kun Ho (1945-), who argued that the Peking Man was a scavenger (Binford and Chuan, 1985), and finally in 1998 to 2004 by a team of computational biologists and anthropologists around Jin Li (金力), who used methods from molecular genetics to demonstrate that the Chinese race, like everyone else too, descended from *homo sapiens* and the African continent in accordance with the 'single-origin hypothesis' (Jin, 1998).

That Chinese dream of racial exclusivity, held mostly by the Han Chinese, didn't differ significantly from that of the British, Germans, Japanese, and Americans before them, and was motivated by a similar desire. Fortunately, it was proven that this theory lacked any scientific evidence. Yet other forms of cultural superiority in Asia remain, such as 'Dahan zhuyi' (大汉族主义, the chauvinistic Han), 'Nihonjin-ron' (日本人論, Japanese uniqueness), the 'Vasudeva' (the supreme man) etc. – all highly complex models not so much of biological, but more of moral or even intellectual superiority (we will come to that later). This superiority has been refflected in party slogans, public policies, and literary movements.

In order to successfully wed man to ideology (again, the concept of 'the one'), not an industrial revolution that manipulates matter, but a cultural revolution that manipulates minds had to take place.

What followed, in the spirit of a neo-Darwinian's 'biologized' society, I call the "husbandry of ideas." This is the notion that ideas can be refined and perfected, just as domestic animals were over the last 2,000 years, by a strict and controlled selection and maintenance process:

如此循环往复，一次比一次更正确，更生动，更丰富。
And so on, over and over again in an endless spiral, with the ideas becoming more correct, more vital and richer each time. (Mao Zedong, 1943; 1967)

The above quote from Mao Zedong sounds ruthless, mainly perhaps because he speaks in his function as a political leader (and known dictator). Who wants to be so openly manipulated by a politician? Nevertheless, what Mao said is essentially at the core of all religious movements and any other mass movement you and I can think of, and, of course, repetition is the very essence of all behavioral modification and psychological conditioning. It is the simple act of value creation. Any personal action causes a result, and that result itself is the truth about the direction and intention of the cause. The repetitive action then constantly confirms our direction and intention. Hence, it does not matter how much a scientist denies the existence of God: As long as some people believe in God, that God is the truth about the cause that leads to Him.

Could the principles of husbandry and selection, which we have seen to be so potent when exercised by a breeder, apply to social and political affairs? They did so in the former Soviet Union and Germany's Nazi government under Hitler; both explicitly used propaganda that favored Communism or Fascism in all forms of media, literary and public expression.

In China's case, we see the systematical ideological indoctrination of Chinese pupils in over 500,000 schools and 1750 universities and colleges till today (2007) during weekly political classes at junior high school and university levels in 毛泽东思想概论 (Thoughts of Mao Zedong), 思想道德修养 (Moral Education), 邓小平理论 (Deng Xiaoping's Theory), 马克思主义哲学原理 (Marxism), 社会主义初级阶段 (Introduction to Socialism), and at primary school level in 思想品德 (Character and Moral Education). Here, the exam results are as crucial for children as the ones in mathematics or physics. Finally, we have the Ministry of Education's 'model scholars' (模范学者) out there virtually proclaiming new Chinese nationalism and unity:

As far as East-West issues are concerned, we practically know the West like the palm of our hand, but the West's vision of the East is a murky confusion. It is thus self-evident who would hold an advantageous position should there be any conflict in the future between the two. (Ji Xianlin in Lin, 1996)

Meanwhile, after jointly winning the Great War in 1948, those self-exiled remnants of European civilization, calling themselves the USA, by now militarily and economically evolved into a European warrior-based culture. They returned to Eurasia and essentially revived Europe, swept through this former cradle of Capitalism, democracy and the free market economy, refined all theories, and built its military and cultural bases all over the place, yet with eyes fixed firmly on the perceived menaces from Asia.

East and West as a result became competitors for better theories, with an Eastern affinity for hyperbole, gigantisms, and holistic totality – the glorification of idols and leaders, state monopolies, authoritarianism, and autarchy: "东方红" ("The East is Red"; Mao Zedong, 1960), which was also the name of the anthem of the Communist Party of China during the 60's and the name of a satellite that carried a radio transmitter broadcasting the song in 1970; and a Western affinity for a historical 'sense of mission' to dissolve and deconstruct the seemingly coherent Eastern cultures and take the lead: "The United States is the locomotive, the rest of the world is the caboose" (Dean Acheson, 1940).

As a result of the Chinese Cultural Revolution (1966-1976), Mao Zedong, in his famous essay "On New Democracy" (新民主主义论, 1964), called it "新的世界革命" or "The New World Revolution." Moreover, during the 'de-Westernization' of Asia and 'de-colonialism' in other parts of the world in the second half of the twentieth century (Han, 1998; Sisci, 2008), the two hemispheres East and West drifted apart, with the remaining inflow of Western ideas and standards (e.g. trials of re-Westernization) often seen as the gongs and drums of a recovering barbarian, more or less until China's opening-up in 1978 and the fall of the communist Soviet Union in 1991.

When Donella H. Meadows' *The Limits to Growth* was published in the USA in 1972 – the first scientific study on the decline of the West that was not purely philosophical and speculative like the theories of Herbert Spencer (1857) and

Arthur Toynbee (1958), but computational and methodical – it became clear to the West that its deduction-based 'materialistic civilization' would one day reach its limits.

Equilibrium

This so-called 'Crisis of the materialistic Civilization' (Meadows, 1972; Husserl, 1970) of the West was supposed to go hand in hand with the 'Revival of the spiritual Civilization' (Kim, 2006), namely the East. In order to prevent our planet's ecological system from ultimate collapse, the deductive-based and nature-abusing West had to learn – so goes Donella Meadows' argument – four important lessons (Meadows, 1972):

i) The world is but one.
ii) The earth is limited, resources are limited, and therefore economic growth is limited.
iii) All the temporal alterations are going in circulation. All phenomena are but alterations rather than developments.

iv)   Human interference with the ecological order will harm nature; balance is needed to maintain universal evolution and harmony in nature.

Needless to say, the four points above neatly correspond to those induction-based, more intuitive Eastern concepts such as 'oneness of heaven and man' (天人合一), 'harmonious society,' 'recurrences in history,' and 'the non-linear concepts of time.' With only two alternatives, the Eastern and Western way, it seems necessary that if the West stopped being Western, it would have to become Eastern. Conversely, that is exactly what the West thought the East was supposed to become, namely a carbon copy of the West.

Meadows' *The Limits to Growth* was published during the Cold War (1950-1989). Imagine the uproar in some Western intellectual circles! Millions of Asians and their sympathizers certainly felt schadenfreude upon hearing that there would be a 'reckoning' for the sins of the Western colonialists, imperialists, and capitalists. Soon, sensationalism on either side prevailed, with media and intellectuals picking up clichés such as 'Confucian Renaissance,' 'the enlightenment of the West towards a more harmonious society,' or the triumph of 'Asian values.' The hasty – if not premature – conclusion of many scholars was this:

The declining West seemed morally bankrupt. That was believable because, like all other human relationships, the East-West relationship should have been based not only on mutual respect (which in this case it never was) but also should have offered the simple lesson of reciprocity, e.g. 'give-and-take' or 'for every gain there is a loss,' or 'baoying' (报应, retribution), or just 'good or bad karma.' But with its attitude of divide, conquer and rule, the West had simply gone too far (Spencer, 1857).

Ever since the European Enlightenment and the Industrial Revolution, the technologically advanced West subjugated the spiritual Eastern nations and taught them scientific ways, thereby inevitably helping Asia and all other nations to develop (助长) and grow. However, "the teacher had refused to appreciate his pupils," to engage with them, and learn enough in return from their intuitive, induction-based traditions.

We have already mentioned the profound love of learning and respect for traditions in Eastern societies. As a consequence, the teacher-student relationship in Asia has always been far more spiritually important and guided by mutual respect, love, and humility than in Western societies. One can only imagine the emotional abuse Asia – a kind, ancient, proud, and exceptionally intelligent civilization – suffered at the hands of her often unfriendly and very oppressive Western master. This brings to mind the song "Mad World" by Gary Jules:

Made me feel the way that every child should, sit and listen; Went to school and I was very nervous, no one knew me; Hello teacher tell me what's my lesson, look right through me. (Gary Jules, 2006)

Western societies "looked right through" their Eastern pupils; there was simply nothing to learn from "a boy of twelve years old," as General Douglas MacArthur said about the Japanese civilization, "as compared to our own (Western civilization's) development of forty-five years" while testifying in front of the US Senate Committee on "Army and on Foreign Relations" (Shibusawa, 2006).

Now that Meadows' *The Limits to Growth* was published, many Asians believed that the day their Western masters' material growth stagnated would be the day when their faithful

Asian pupils would offer their spiritual advice and wisdom (about harmoniousness, alternative world views, the oneness of nature and man etc.), at least in theory (Toynbee, 1958; Zaehner, 1976; Thoreau, 1988; Ji, 2006). The very opposite occurred, of course.

In practice, as we all know, economic growth – although more or less stagnant in Western Europe and America – is still rampant and plentiful in the developing parts of 'Westernized' Asia, albeit with the looming presence of Western companies and corporate money. The West, it seems, isn't exhausted as long as there are still growth opportunities, overseas markets, and material resources to lay its hands on. Therefore, in this twenty-first century, in Asia some are still asking the same question they asked in the 1970's: When will Asian values or belief systems finally start to have a measurable impact on those Western invaders, and, even more important: Will the East be able to 'give' as much as it is able to 'take' in (Wu, 2007)?

Evidence shows the East has some influence on the West. A strengthening of the East is already in the making, although the deduction-based narcissist West, which got itself lost, to use the words of Aby-Lughod, in a universe of "vulgar and utterly finicky, atomistic details," for the time being is unable to see through the natural greater scheme of things (Ng, 1998; Wu, 1997, 1998; Wallerstein, 2005; Chirot, 1991; Aby-Lughod, 1989). Similarly, the 'white West' failed to anticipate its ethnic suicide (Heinsohn, 2003, 2005) and its failure (or the failure of its economic and social theories) to predict the rise of East Asia (Lin, 2006).

For, in having been able to resist Western imperialism and colonialism – above all a moral victory – and easily forming by far the most populous nations on the 'world island,' Asia now accounts for 65 percent of the world's population and Europe for only 11 percent. With contempt for Western aggression and, in the case of Russia and China, no longer intimidated by the Western powers, Asiacentrism in geopolitical terms had set in after the 1950's – in my estimation long before the two giants, China and India, had their respective economies (c. 1990-2007) to prove it.

Today's de-Westernization is not only taking place in obvious places like China, Japan, Russia, Korea etc., but also in the Middle East, Africa, and South-East Asia. Many people have serious doubts about the West, its intentions and deeply flawed views. Ultranationalist bestsellers like *The Japan That Can Say*

No (1989) by Akio Morita and Shintaro Ishihara, and *China Can Say No* (1996) by Song Qiang (宋强) are among the milder ones of their kind, both strongly opposing the Caucasian world order and Western values (Morita, 1989; Song, 1996). Why should Japanese culture bow down to the whims of America's corporate culture? Why don't China and India with their histories of 5,000 years and combined population of 2.5 billion resist this pre-adolescent monkey business of the USA with regards to teaching Asia a lesson in human rights, democracy, and statecraft? After all, the USA 'preemptively' bombed the Middle East and tortured 'enemy combatants' at Guantanamo Bay Detention Camp on the shore of Cuba (Human Rights Watch, 2003; Amnesty International, 2005).

Remarkably, the East-West dichotomy, as if an invisible hand has dealt the right cards, still determines world affairs and history despite long and enduring phases of centrism, trials of expansion, colonialism and empire, alliances and ganging-ups, rivalry and false beliefs in superiority. What makes us think then that the disparity of East and West can be best explained by anything other than a law of nature? Is there a scientific 'dualism' similar to the one recognized by Valentinovich G. Plekhanov (1856-1918), founder of 'dialectical materialism,' who says that science entails contradictions inherited in all natural and social phenomena called 'laws of dialectics' [science of contradictions] (Plekhanov, 1891)? Is there are law of 'difference' similar to Jacques Derrida's (1930-2004) concept of 'différance' suggested in his masterpiece *De La Grammatologie* (1967), in which he argued that the prime function of all languages and thoughts is 'differing' – the 'differentiation' of signs from each other (Derrida, 1967)?

As for common sense, a people's good intentions, or bad ones, are useless when it comes to interfering with scientific laws. If there is a scientific reason behind why the omnipotent West never wanes, yet on the other hand, despite countless trials of conquest, colonialism, and intimidation, never turned the East into the West either… doesn't this suggest the very dichotomy of East and West is essentially a natural trait of the human race? Is there a law of nature that pushed East and West in diametrically opposed directions, making one become more inductive, and the other more deductive, while keeping both hemispheres in balance?

Alas, no humanist wants to hear a theory that equates the evolution of our precious *homo sapiens* with the development of a dualism that somehow achieved a perfect East-West equilibrium. The day we discover such a rare dualistic creature in the animal kingdom, however, might change all that.

Until then, in order to answer those questions, some key areas can be discussed in which a possible unintended yet synchronized behavior of the integration-based East and analysis-based West has clearly played a role in keeping a relative equilibrium during the last 50 years of 'catching-up-with-the-West' Asiacentrism.

Demography

Why are the people thus busily moving?
For food they are seeking, children they fain would beget,
feeding them all as they can.
Traveler, mark this well, and when thou art home, do thou likewise!
More can no mortal effect, work with what ardor he will.
(Johann W. von Goethe, 1790)

With the decline of Europe during the Great War, the multiethnic USA survived as the only counterweight to the overwhelmingly racially homogeneous countries of the East: China was 92 percent ethnic Han, Nippon was 99 percent ethnic Japanese, and Korea was 99 percent ethnic Korean. Meanwhile, the (coherently perceived) Muslim world, the Hindu world, and the Soviet empire together comprised over two billion people. During the next few decades of reconstructing Europe, all major Eastern cultures, often driven by political utopian dreams, increased their populations so dramatically as if to prove Thomas Malthus (1766-1834) wrong:

中国人口众多是一件极大的好事。再增加多少倍人口也完全有办法，这办法就是生产.
The massive population of China is our greatest good. Even a further increase of several times the population is entirely possible, possible through productivity.
(Mao Zedong, 1960, Vol. 4)

Thomas Malthus, an English philosopher, made his famous prediction in "An Essay on the Principle of Population" (1798) that population growth would at some point in time outrun food supply, and hence that the world population must have a maximum limit of between nine to twelve billion. Naturally, until that final limit is reached, some nations would try, almost fanatically as in the case of Maoist China until the early 80's, or not try at all, as in case of post-war Germany after the 50's, which officially discouraged children, to outperform each other – for instance by forbidding contraception, ruling out gay communions, encouraging matchmaking, rewarding 'patriotic' baby-making, or discouraging women from joining the labor force (Heinsohn, 2003 [1]). Japan's population increased from 60 to 127 million, India from 550 to 1100 million, China exploded in population from 600 to over one billion and 350 million, the citizens of the Soviet Union grew from 100 million to 450 million (by annexation), and finally the entire Arab/Moslem population almost tripled to one billion 400 million (with Indonesia from 75 to 220 million, Pakistan from 39 to 167 million etc.) (*GeoHive*, 2008; *CIA Factbook*, 2008).

As I write this paper, the populations of China and India have each increased by 20 million in the past 18 months, close to the size of that of Australia. That is of course a far cry from back in the year 2000, when China reported 36 million 'millennium babies' (*China Daily*, 2012/02/01). By modern European standards, such figures are utopian and utterly mind-boggling. And it does not stop here: In 2007, in just one of its 22 provinces, namely in Henan, China saw a birthrate of roughly 1.2 million Chinese babies, some 500,000 more than entire Germany in that same year – however, 28 percent of the 'German babies' were of non-German ethnic descent (destasis, 2006). Tens of thousand million babies is a post-modern sin, even for a proud and wise civilization like China. So, Henan's local authorities, in order to counter their outrageously high birthrate of 1.6 million annually during the 90's, had to promise Beijing not to exceed the province's projected population of 110 million before the year 2020 (*China Daily*, 2008/04/20). Hurray to that! To put this into perspective: During the Olympic Year in Beijing in 2008, 20 million Chinese were born in mainland China. And this, despite the 'one-child policy' from 1979, although heavily relaxed, still being in place (there are many exceptions to the policy, and minorities and rich folks are exempted anyway, but we won't go into that here). Growing at this rate, the world's entire World War II casualties (roughly 72 million people, including all casualties of famine!) are replaced by China alone in a little under four years. Add the babies from India, Pakistan, and Bangladesh, and the World War II losses are remedied in just under 18 months. In this context, Darwin's words sound ironic:

In this case we can clearly see that if we wished in imagination to give the plant the power of increasing in number, we should have to give it some advantage over its competitors. (Charles Darwin, 1859 [2])

However, in the short run between the years 1950 and 2000, the doctrine of Darwin (and, in politics, Marx) had disappointed the people, and so did the practice of Social Darwinism as a nominal imperative: Numbers (and mind you, it is always about numbers!) of citizens did not immediately translate into global dominance. Something rather counter-intuitive happened, as the believed outcome of the struggle for survival against the West failed to materialize:

> *If two great regions had been for a long period favorably circumstanced in an equal degree, the battle would be prolonged and severe; [...]. But in the course of time, the forms dominant in the highest degree, wherever produced, would tend everywhere to prevail. As they prevailed, they would cause the extinction of other and inferior forms, [...].* (Charles Darwin, 1859 [3])

What Darwin had anticipated for the plants and animal kingdom, namely that biological mass or discipline (instinct) of a group leads to victory, seemed technically absurd: Although the Caucasian population in the USA, Great Britain, Germany, and France declined in relation to most other great Asian nations, these countries assimilated quite well the mass migration from East to West. On the contrary, the West was able to profit from its newly won diversity, calling it 'multiculturalism,' the only 'minor' problem being that of successful integration: Already in the year 2007, in Amsterdam, the capital of The Netherlands, almost 40 percent of its 750,000 inhabitants were ethnic minorities, and 60 percent of children in primary schools were of non-Dutch descent. The influx of Asians, and also of Eastern Europeans and Africans, had made a great impact on the USA, the European Union, Canada, Australia, and other Western countries, which also led to pressure as these immigrants often have more children than the domestic populations (Heinsohn, 2005).

Soon, critics were wielding clichés such as 'moral conquerors' and 'spiritual invasion' (Freytag, 1940; 2004), 'Counter-Colonialism,' 'the Gradual Orientalization of the Western Culture' and 'Pacific Century,' meaning that the twenty-first century will be dominated by the Pacific Rim states, including China, Japan, and the USA (Gibney, 1992; PBS, 1993; Borthwick, 1998), 'The Chinese Enlightenment of the West,' 'Eastern takeover' or 'Clash of Civilizations' (Huntington, 1993; 2000; 2004). All these notions, supported by popular academic data, suggest that conformist East Asians and individualistic Westerners – apart from having shaped two entirely different civilizations, one induction-based, the other deduction-based – indeed seem to produce different general cognitive styles too.

The latter tend to reason more analytically, the former tend to reason more holistically (Masuda & Nisbett, 2001).

The demographic changes in Europe are irreversible, and the former feelings of Western superiority – the analytical mind, the linear approach to time and history, the soul of the conqueror, the deductive ways – over time will proportionally decrease in favor of a newly felt Eastern superiority – the intuitive mind, the holistic approach to time, the *non-Western experience* of history, the soul of the sage, the inductive ways.

As a matter of perception, till today, the Western ways are universally associated with 'war', 'aggression,' and 'exclusiveness,' while the Eastern ways are associated with 'peace,' 'tranquility,' and 'inclusiveness' – notwithstanding both hemispheres showing the tendencies to project their own psychological outlook onto the other. For the vast majority of Americans and Europeans, Asia is a place for all those fanatics, dictators, terrorists, and immature cultures. For the Asians, the West – despite its cruelties and flaws – is often seen as the savior who brings stability, happiness, and peace to the world.

As a consequence of 'psychological projection,' the West does not clearly see its own vices, and the East does not clearly see its own virtues.

Due to current demographic developments, Europe is going to change and will have to accept more of the Eastern inductive ways. Or does it? It will take some time, to say the least. The non-integrated, non-secular Muslims in Germany, Austria, and The Netherlands still feel they are second-class citizens: As a minority, they are not alone in Europe (*Times*, 2008/07/27; *taz*, 2008/02/12). In Great Britain, France, Spain, and Italy, too, most of their Muslim, Asian or East Asian counterparts (may they be Turks, Algerians, Chinese, Sikhs etc., who will anyway represent 53 percent of the European population in the year 2100) still report they are having a hard time adjusting to the – from their perspective – very limited way of Western thinking. Many Eastern immigrants, including most Europeans themselves, believe that European culture has killed the Indians, developed slavery, colonized and exploited the Third World, brought war and misery to the human cause, and should thus disappear from the surface of the Earth, obviously not by war, but by silent assimilation. In Berlin, it is not uncommon for a white German woman to be labeled 'snobbish' or even plain 'racist' just because she chooses a white German partner, instead of showing her 'tolerance' by choosing a non-white spouse. It has become, in the language of the youth, "hip" in Europe to "go non-white."

The new spiritual conquerors, with their Eastern religions, values, and world views, as well as their inductive ways are demanding more power and influence in their host countries of choice, and they are lobbied by approximately three billion other Indians, Chinese, Muslims, South-East Asians etc. While Europe and North America are volunteering to 'transform' their indigenous cultures, China, India, Singapore, Hong Kong, and others are all happy to assimilate those few (relative in number) 'Western runners.' Westerners hardly ever call themselves immigrants; they prefer the exclusive, high-status term 'expatriates' or 'expats' while abroad who turn their backs on their deconstructed, apparently moribund civilization, and search for refuge in the strong and massive Eastern hemisphere. But, alas, despite finding themselves admired and useful due to their deductive, analytical ways and deconstructive skills, as lone individuals they have an impact no less but also no greater than a water drop in the vast sea of Eastern inclusive 'harmoniousness' and universal 'oneness.'

In the short run, the few young indigenous Europeans who have not yet immigrated into the Anglo-Saxon world (Heinsohn,

2003; Breithaupt, 2000) or found some purpose in the East, will stay on their home turf and indeed benefit from their continent's accumulated wealth, with fewer and fewer people sharing that wealth. In the long term, however, their parents, companies, and governments will have to make a painful but crucial financial decision:

There is nothing complicated about finance. It is based on old people lending to young people. [...]. Never before in human history, though, has a new generation simply failed to appear. (David P. Goldman, 2008/05)

The aging Europeans' search for their 'next generation,' may it be citizens for their cities, tenants for their houses, consumers, students, employees, spouses, or just new ideas, has already begun – they look to the East.

Whoever said that "victory makes you liberal while defeat makes you conservative" must have had an in-depth understanding of the laws of sociology. The Europeans in the twenty-first century are suffering from low birth rates, defenselessness, and dependency, and thus have developed a pervasive fear of everything Asian. Does this new twenty-first century existential angst resemble that old twentieth-century existential angst, so accurately portrayed in images of the "Yellow Terror" such as Wilhelm II.'s painting *Völker Europas, Wahrt Eure Heiligsten Güter* (*People of Europe, Safeguard Your Most Valuable Goods*), which depicts the European nations standing on a cliff guarding against a mighty Buddha and his thunderstorm (Wikipedia, 2008)? Or as exemplified by the short stories written at the end of the nineteenth century by Matthew Phipps Shiel, who brutally familiarized Westerners with the term *The Yellow Peril*? How about the fear of Islamic Extremists? Or the fear of mass immigration out of Africa and the Middle East? Is there anything in this century that Europeans are *not* afraid of? Does this new twenty-first century existential angst resemble the old pessimism of an Oswald Spengler or an Arnold Toynbee, both of whom summarized angst in their *The Decline of the West* (1918) and *Civilization on Trial and the World and the West* (1958)? How about the paranoid 'angst' of a Willhelm Marr in his *Finis Germania*, a manifesto about the decline of the Germanic race(s) to which also the Anglo-Saxons belong (Marr, 1879; Heihnson, 2006; Fülberth, 2007). If angst still reigns over Europe, it comes as no surprise that the Christian Democratic Union and the Christian Social Union of Bavaria in Germany have published their "Asia-Strategy Paper" (October 23, 2007), which officially labels China a "threat to European values, economic and political development" (Schröder, 2008; *Spiegel*, 2008/07/15). Is that paper reflecting mere diplomatic foolishness, the insecurity of its authors, or does it just smell like honest, genuine fear? Presumably, it is a bit of all and shows that Germany is spiritually on the retreat. She is not prepared to compromise her Western values, despite the fact that 98 percent of humankind is not German, would not want to join Germany or be labeled German, and already regards the Chinese as Europe's valuable economic and political partners, not as a threat. But the above example gives us an idea of the 'psychology of failure' (in this case, two world wars) and the wish to stand up for something meaningful again, in this case for 'Western values,' while at the same time discrediting or even denying such a thing as 'Asian values.' That this entails rendering all non-Western societies as inferior or immature, does not and will never come naturally to Germany's cultural mind, if you recall European history – and especially eighteenth-, nineteenth-, and twentieth-century German Orientalism (Marchand, 2001). Anything close to a 'revolution of the spirit,' a change of attitude towards China on the part of Germany (or any other European society for that matter), must come first and foremost from within the *heart*. In this case, it comes from the blending of Eastern and Western spirits that slowly sink into the hearts and minds of the European people. In reality it's all happening through the physical migration of more and more Easterners into the European heartland.

In the latter half of the twentieth century and in this century, the new spiritual strength of the integration-based Orient, derived from the explosion in population, manifested itself in a new self-confidence and assertiveness and the re-affirmation of (superior) Asian values and pan-Asianism, the old notion that Asia indeed is the unifying 'one,' while the West is the destructive 'other':

> *[...] that broad expanse of love for the Ultimate and Universal, which is the common thought-inheritance of every Asiatic race, enabling them to produce all the great religions of the world, and distinguishing them from those maritime peoples of the Mediterranean and the Baltic, who love to dwell on the Particular, and to search out the means, not the end, of life.* (Okakura Kakuzo, 1904)

> *[...] no description of Hinduism can be exhaustive which does not touch on almost every religious and philosophical idea that the world has ever known...*
> (M. Monier Williams, 1894)

[...] It is all-tolerant, all-compliant, all-comprehensive, all-absorbing. (S. Radhakrishnan, 1929)

[...] European culture has the ability to master energy and mechanics, but has only elementary knowledge regarding the human body and the concert of mind and brain. The Middle and the Far East (however) have an advance of thousand years on the West. (Claude Lévi-Strauss, 1952)

The modern idea of 'pan-Asianism' and the slogan "Asia is one" were first discussed in Okakura Kakuzo's groundbreaking book *The Ideals of the East* (1904), but became really popular again in the nineties during the academic discourse on 'Asian values': 'Asian values' is a vague concept of certain religious and spiritual tendencies, traditions, and virtues like filial piety, love of learning, collectivism, and inner-world dependency that are shared by most Asian (some say only Confucian) cultures, but are not – or not equally – stressed in most Western societies (Han, 1998). By definition, Asian values form a self-affirming psychological counterpoise, and thus conflict with those Western values of Judeo-Christian historical revelations, liberalism, individualism, and dependency on the outer world.

Another major blow to Western hubris was the genetic challenge. According to *The Wall Street Journal,* "American-Asian minorities make up three point five percent of the country's population, but they account for more than twenty to thirty percent of students in America's top universities" (Golden, 2006; 2011), and since the 1920's, the beginnings of research on race differences, it has been known, and has been proven independently by psychologists such as Jean Philippe Rushton and Arthur Robert Jensen (2006), Richard Herrnstein and Charles Murray (1994), James Robert Flynn (1980; 1994), and Ian Deary (2001), among others, that East Asians on average do score six to seven points higher than Anglo-Americans, and 20 points higher than Afro-Americans on most (Western-) standardized intelligence tests (Rushton et. al., 2006; Herrnstein et. al., 1994; Flynn, 1980, 1994; Deary, 2001; Steinberg, 1994). This is readily available science; no one is in the dark any longer. Indeed, the cognitive preeminence of East Asians in several intellectual and artistic disciplines is as fascinating and terrifying to look at as, for instance, watching the awesome dominance of Afro-American basketball players in the National Basketball Association (Flynn, 1994; Ledderose, 2005).

When we combine the high test results of East Asians with student numbers, we get even more impressive results: In the year 2005, China, still offically a developing country, announced it had 19 million undergraduate and graduate students enrolled on the mainland, without Hong Kong and Taiwan (CNET, 2005/08/30). Great Britain, in the same year, had hardly 2.3 million students, of whom 300,000 were foreign nationals, over 51,000 of them ethnic Chinese (BBC, 2007/03/27).

The cultural and economic penalty for not recognizing Asian talent is immense, and it therefore comes as no surprise that in this century, we have witnessed in particular the Anglophone world recruiting Chinese and Indian students in unprecedented numbers. In the year 2005, 65,000 Chinese and 75,000 Indians studied in the USA; and 60,000 Chinese and 20,000 Indians in Great Britain (IIE, 2006; *People's Daily*, 2006/04/05). In the record year of 2012, it was estimated that 157,558 Chinese students attended school in the USA (Mellman, 2012). By comparison, when we look at American students studying in China, that number had barely reached 14,000 this year (Siow, 2012), many of whom are American-Chinese or 'hai gui' (海龟, sea turtles). With this trend of recruiting more Asian talent came 'political correctness' and the need to talk about differences in *culture* and *cultural values* (e.g. Fukuyama, Huntington etc.), rather than differences in *race* and *phenotypes* (e.g. Herrnstein, Flynn etc.):

> *Genetic differences among individual human beings account for up to eighty-five percent of the entire genetic spectrum, while the genetic differences in the world population are only about fifteen percent. No matter which ethnic group you come from, we're all pretty much the same.* (Jin Li [金力], 2006)

To conclude, in discussing demography, 'cultural evolution' is so much better to explain group differences than her abusive father, 'Biological Evolution,' and her damaged mother, 'Social Evolution.' The huge transformation of key Western societies into fissiparous, multicultural hubs fits the equation of the East-West equilibrium as a global theory: Migration is in direct reciprocity, for the greater good, a strategy of mutual cooperation and – unconsciously, but we'd rather say voluntary – the natural response to any human demographic shortcomings on this planet. Without having to care about race, by carefully only talking about *culture,* Western ranks are slowly but steadily being filled with the surplus of human capital produced by Eastern societies – as diverse as possible, please. It serves both hemispheres, and thus benefits the equilibrium: The analytical, deductive West increases its diversity, tendency for devolution, and multiculturalism, and is thus profiting from Eastern 'overproduction' of human capital that is required to keep Western culture alive, while the integration-based East increases its ethnic dominance and geopolitical reach (politicians call it "soft power"), thereby forcing ever greater levels of peace, tolerance, and harmoniousness onto the West.

Migration

As a rule, any society that is single-mindedly interested in its own promotion and thus in the survival and preservation of its culture would have to have a huge population and send its people out, not letting too many others in.

The European nation states send a lot of people out, but do not have huge populations, and let everyone in. The USA has a huge population, but sends not enough people out, and lets everyone in. Japan has a big population (twice the size of Great Britain or France), lets no one in, and sends few out. China, India, and the Islamic world come very close to the ideal of a society that has the means to let its culture survive for a very long time.

Cultural Effects of the Dichotomy

In 1275, Marco Polo famously reported about Cathay's (China) pompous cities, stupendous power, and incredible wealth (Pelliot & Moule, 1938). But the first encounters of scale and cultural significance between East and West were the many Jesuit missions during the late Ming Dynasty. Indeed, Matteo Ricci (1552-1610), Francis Xavier (1505-1552), and Jean Adam Schall von Bell (1519-1566), like most other Jesuit missionaries in Asia, came, saw, and wrote extensively about the Chinese civilization that – despite its numerous follies and shortcomings – in many ways was not only superior in size and number. Its people were also "more polite, delicate and gentle in nature," and thus outclassed the West not only "in scope of its economies" and in terms of its "sympathetic, true human intelligence" (Gu, 1922), but also in its awareness of its sophisticated moral code and perceived antiquity (Hart, 1999):

It is a well-known fact that the liking – you may call it the taste for the Chinese – grows upon the foreigner the longer he lives in this country. (Gu Hongming, 1922)

Despite the achievements of the Jesuits in China in the seventeenth century, one should not merely attribute their successes to the curiosity of the Chinese intellectuals, or to the expertise and advanced scientific training of the Catholic Church, but perhaps more so to the cosmopolitan mind of China's emperors. It was not uncommon for the 'Shangdi' (Emperor) to employ foreigners (Li, 1998). For example, it was the Shunzhi Emperor (顺治帝, 1638-1661) who promoted Cologne-born German Jesuit Johann Adam Schall von Bell to a Mandarin of first class; and it was the Kangxi Emperor (康熙帝, 1654-1722) who frequently summoned the Vlaanderen-born Belgian Ferdinand Verbiest (1623-1688) to the Forbidden City (紫禁城). Shunzhi and Kangxi both were keen on having the Jesuits bring new science and technology to China, not necessarily because they felt China was desperately in need of Western technology, but because that was what vassal states were supposed to do in those days of 'tianxia' (天下, The Celestial Empire or All under Heaven): The non-Chinese scholars, disarmed and mesmerized by the immense power and might of the Chinese civilization, out of humbleness and submission, were simply *expected* to (and really felt obliged to) contribute to the Empire and in return were rewarded privileges and official posts *quid pro quo*.

"It is power that makes one benevolent" – that same kind of fair-minded atmosphere of tolerance, academic freedom, and mutual dependency during the Ming Dynasty would have been difficult to achieve in nitpicking, prejudiced Europe. Or can anybody imagine the impossible scenario of some Chinese Daoist monks walking into Vatican City of the Dark Ages and negotiating alternative world views with the clerics? Not even the Church's own people, not even the Jesuits could do that, if one recalls Galileo Galilei (1564-1642), who happened to spend the latter part of his life under inquisitional house arrest.

Thus, I imagine the Jesuits had an extraordinarily good time in Asia while living under 'tianxia,' built some churches but also translated Chinese literature, and respected the Confucian code of moral conduct and learning, in exchange for an equally curious and tolerant Chinese audience (Li, 1998; Jami, 2001).

With wave after wave of Jesuits flocking into China, embracing the Chinese, and 'mysteriously' turning into 'apostles of Confucius' (Hart, 1999), it is not difficult to understand why, in 1704, Pope Clement XI finally intervened and issued his notorious papal bull, condemning all Chinese beliefs and rites *per se*. It was outrageous and plainly inconceivable to the Catholic Church "how a system of filial piety and state morality called Confucian could take the place of a proper religion, could make men, even the mass of Asia, do without religion" (Gu, 1922). Of course, the fascination with Chinese culture would never decrease in Western academic circles. It could only increase.

The Germans admired Asia immensely. Johann Wolfgang von Goethe rejoiced: "They have another peculiarity; in China men and nature are inseparable." Gottfried Wilhelm Leibniz wrote that this by far most populous nation on Earth, with a highly ordered civil structure, must have achieved that population and civil structure through some identifiable means. Satirically, Leibniz suggested that Chinese missionaries should be invited to instruct the European people (Cook & Rosemont, 1994).

After two opium wars, the British imperialists of those days – otherwise totally convinced of their new 'religion' of *Anglo-Saxon Capitalism* and *industrial superiority* – nevertheless still found occasional sufficient praise for their 'conquered.' In 1922, after spending a year lecturing at Peking University, the British philosopher and mathematician Bertrand Russell, despite his ludicrous criticism of the "cowardice, callousness, and voraciousness in the average Chinaman," still found mostly words of admiration for China's cultural industrialism and overeager hospitality (Chinese intellectuals literally bent over backwards to please foreigners, and treated Russell courteously), and, naturally, the Imperial examination system (c. 605-1905) or 'ke ju' [科举] (Russell, 1922). This gargantuan system of totalitarian proportion yet universal meritocracy (in theory, but in practice there is abuse in any system) had, over the course of 1,300 years, co-shaped Confucian China and Imperial China, and, although formally abandoned in 1905, in Russell's time still dominated people's minds and attitudes towards learning and career. The Imperial system, unlike the European one of those days, was theoretically blind to the social class or creed of its candidates, and was solely designed to find the most intelligent and diligent contenders among the huge Chinese gene pool.

Russell's analysis of China and its people concludes with a prophecy, namely that the Chinese civilization alone has the power to easily supersede, both economically and intellectually, all European states combined if only they adopt Western science to defend themselves against aggression, but otherwise stay faithful to their own fine civilization (Russell, 1922). For those who did not believe in China's potential 'other' civilization, Russell had this warning:

The Chinese demand Western science. But they do not demand the adoption of the Western philosophy of life. If they were to adopt the Western philosophy of life, they would, as soon as they had made themselves safe against foreign aggression, embark upon aggression on their own account. (Bertrand Russell, 1922)

Unfortunately, to this day, this is exactly what half-educated Western policymakers encourage China to become. Ignoring any information about China is not knowledge about China. With their often reckless demands for 'The American Dream,' the 'Rechts- und Verfassungsstaat,' 'Democracy,' and 'Human Rights,' the Western nations of today are aiming at establishing a Middle Kingdom in their own image: "Hey, China, you look like one of us. Look what we've made you!"

Two Successful Models

Despite evidence for the 'other humanity' in the East, a civilization that went down the inductive path, ship after ship of enthusiastic but ignorant Western scholars set their sails for Asia, their eyes fixed on analyzing and deconstructing the hype and propaganda of 'the exotic Other' and proving that the East is a mere repressed, introverted Sleeping Beauty, denying the existence of the East-West dichotomy, ignoring all warnings, only to discover the same old truth over and over again: The East constitutes an entirely different type of humanity. It is holistic, non-analytical, and spiritual – it is integration-based, and it is very capable and strong. We come back to that in a minute. But first some more facts:

Most sinologists and universal historians today more or less agree that before Xu Guangqi (徐光启, 1562-1633) published his translation of the first six books of Euclid's *Elements of Geometry* in 1607, this kind of Greek/Hellenistic, analytic-deductive driven mathematics and axiomatic proof-findings had been systematically unknown to Asia (Needham, 1964; Hart, 1999; Spence, 2001). Indeed, it took China's mathematicians roughly 250 years, until in 1851 Alexander Wylie (1815-1887) and Li Shanlan (李善兰, 1811-1882) published the second half of the translation of Euclid's *Elements of Geometry*, to realize the practicability of axioms at all (Horng & Wann-Sheng, 2001).

What started off as cooperation between Xu Guangqi and Matteo Ricci in 1607 later became the nucleus of an entirely new branch of Western scholarship – 'The History of Science in China.' Why is that such an interesting new branch of scholarship? Well, since it was European missionaries who proactively entered China and taught the Chinese, not some Chinese missions to Europe, and since the Western missionaries were believed to possess the religion of truth and analytical sciences, how was it possible that an atheistic, non-analytical civilization like China nevertheless had developed into an intelligent, fully-functional society that in countless fields like art, agriculture, astronomy, economics, logistics, medicine, and mechanics was more advanced than its European counterparts? That is why the 'History of Science in China' had to be carefully reconstructed in the West in order to make sense of it all; the only problem was that Western scholars translated almost all of China's socio-cultural originality – its concepts and non-European ideas – into convenient European taxonomies (a fascinating topic and text-book case of cultural imperialism which unfortunately we cannot discuss in detail here).

The Jesuits in China, as I said elsewhere before, were mostly successful simply because they did not insist on forcing the whole of Eurocentric catechism on the ordinary Chinaman; on the contrary, they even adapted to Confucian scholarship. However, what they reported back to Europe about the kind, good-hearted, intelligent, and confident Chinaman and his unique state morality and Confucian/Daoism/Buddhism mode of conduct often nurtured a certain dislike for the 'second humanity.' In comparison to Muhammad's teachings in the *Quran*, which is after all a relatively young religious canon (c. 600), Islam is essentially dogmatic but practical, thus having turned into a physical competitor, whereas the much older *I Ching* (易经, c. 1050 BC-256 BC), *Dao De Jing* (道德经, c. 600 BC), the Buddhist sutras (佛经, c. 500 BC), or *The Analects* (论

语, ca. 479 BC-221 BC) seem to cover deeply philosophical issues, metaphysics, difficult mathematics, and a complex moral system, much of it posing some serious challenges to some of those ambivalent wisdom offered in the Bible. In other words, Christianity had found some sort of enlightened competitor.

The German philosopher Friedrich Schelling (1775-1854) was convinced that already in prehistoric times, China became unique, 'the other humanity,' distinct from the rest of the world, and, furthermore, that is was the only living remnant of a time before the world was divided into two different humanities (Schelling, 1842). He also branded China "un univers sans Dieu." Johann Gottfried Herder (1744-1803) labeled it "an embalmed mummy wound in silk" and the Chinese "corner people." Finally, Alain Peyrefitte (1925-1999), author of *The Collision of Two Civilizations*, famously called it "l'empire immobile" (Bernie, 2005) because of its compliance and, ultimately, meekness.

Same Europeans who believed in God and the scientific ways, sensing a lack both of religion and science in China, assumed there had been no scientific advancement in China before the Europeans arrived. Not quite a fair observation, as we know today. It is true that before the introduction of Western sciences, there had been indeed no need for foreign axioms. But that was simply because East Asia had cultivated its own practical brand of mathematics, primarily relying on induction and analogical reasoning. In fact, this stubborn and very different 'scientific' approach of the Chinese has infuriated the European Imperialists ever since, culminating in the famous, almost hysterical saying by Sir Reverant Arthur Smith in *The Chinese Characteristics* (1890) that "the Chinese mind absolutely must be algebraic, while the Western mind is arithmetical" (Smith, 1890).

The Chinese Characteristics, mainly because of its style, is probably the single most outrageous book on the peculiarities of the Chinaman ever written, causing waves of anti-Western resentment among the Chinese leading up to the Boxer Rebellion against the Western imperialists at the turn of the nineteenth century (1899-1901). Yet, Smith simply recounted what every scientist in the field already knew: There is the integration-based East, and there is the analysis-based West, and no third mode of reasoning other than that of the inductive and deductive modes has ever been achieved by human beings. It seemed incredible, but here was Asia, which excelled more in the inductive ways, and there was Europe, which excelled more in the deductive ways. And that was it.

Gems of ancient Chinese inductive-driven mathematics are: *The Book of Changes* [易经], written during the Zhou Dynasty (1050 BC-256 BC, possibly originated around 2800 BC by Fu Xi [伏羲]); the *Book of Poetry* [诗经] with pieces written around the year 1000 BC; the *Mo Jing* [墨经] (470 BC-390 BC); *The Nine Chapters on the Mathematical Art* [九章算术] (c. 200 BC-AD 179). Here I should add that *The Nine Chapters* had a great influence on the Japanese scholar Seki Takakazu who developed – during the Edo Period (1603-1867) – another arithmetical, idiosyncratic mathematics called 'wasan' (和算). Other valuable works on Chinese mathematics include the *Zhoubi Manual* [周髀算经] written during the Han period (c. 202 BC-AD 220); the *Sea Island Manual* [海岛算经] written during the Three Kingdoms period in the year 263; and the *Jade Mirror of the Four Unknowns* [四元玉监] written in 1303. Zhu Shijie [朱世杰] (1303) once said, in the tradition of *The Book of Changes*: "'One' is the source of all mathematics" and that those words of the *Dao De Jing* (道德经, c. 600 BC): "The Dao begets the One; the One begets the Two opposites" really summarize (Chinese) mathematics: "All stems from the number 'one.'" By this, Zhu

Shijie perfectly harmonized Chinese mathematics with the Eastern concept of 'oneness,' thus once more effectively defining the essence and story of most Eastern 'philosophies' – be it the teachings of Siddhartha Buddha (563 BC-483 BC), Vyasa of the *Mahabharata* (c. 800 BC), or the *Four Confucian Classics* (四書五經, before 221 BC).

Someone who is genuinely interested in mathematics may as well call the cited works above the "Chinese Computation Classics." Xu Guangqi made some genuine attempts to integrate Western and Chinese mathematics, but ended up being all too pragmatic about it – if a Chinese equation led to the same result as Western mathematics did, it was there to stay, if not, it was to be abandoned (Engelfriet & Siu, 2001).

Chinese mathematics, which had a great influence on mathematics in Korea and Japan as well, flourished until approximately the twelfth and thirteenth centuries, fell into decline after the arrival of the Jesuits and Westerners and their teachings about arithmetical mathematics and science, and became almost forgotten during the nineteenth and twentieth centuries (Jami et al., 2001; Engelfriet & Siu, 2001). But that does not necessarily mean that it was all 'no good' – on the contrary:

Zhu Shijie, in his *Jade Mirror*, for example, teaches a diagram similar to that in Blaise Pascal's *Traité du triangle arithmétique*, the latter of which was not published until 1665 in Europe. Why had the world waited 362 years for Pascal's triangle when Zhu Shijie's diagram could have initiated the same mathematical revolution? A convincing answer to that is given in the Study of the *Fourteenth-Century Manual on Polynomial Equations* by John Hoe:

> *Chinese written language enabled Chinese mathematicians to express themselves with a conciseness that is almost impossible to attain in highly-inflected natural languages, using an alphabet, such as prevailed in Europe. Thus, Chinese were able to deal with problems which in the West could not be tackled until a suitable mathematical symbolism had been developed. At the same time, this meant that the Chinese mathematicians never had the incentive to develop a fully symbolic algebraic notation, since the need for one was never as acutely felt as in Europe.* (John Hoe, 2007)

Language barriers, cultural prejudices, ignorance, or pure spite? Most likely, these were all factors, among others. In this regard, not a lot has changed in the last 400 years. Don't expect many American or European citizens, even the more educated ones, to master their host country's language or to know anything about their host country other than the information they have obtained from English-language sources and textbooks. It is not going to happen; it is wishful thinking. As the German-Swiss writer Hermann Hesse once wrote: "We cannot and we must not become Chinese, and at heart we don't want to either. We must not seek ideal or higher meaning of life in China or in any other thing of the past; otherwise we lose ourselves and adhere to a fetish" (Hesse, 1921).

Already in 1627, Xu Guangqi [徐光启] applied scientific methods and conducted experiments – as demonstrated in the vast corpus of his works leading to his *Almanac of Agriculture* (农政全书, 1627) – on crops, sweet potatoes, and water irrigation, to name but a few (Jami, 2001). The results were impressive. In 1630, China could feed its 70 million people. Some 120 years later, when Great Britain was forced to think scientifically about how to improve her agriculture in order to feed her 'overpopulation' of some 5.7 million, China was already feeding a nation of roughly 200 million.

Similarly, the *Chinese Traditional Calendar* by Guo Shoujing (郭守敬, 1231-1316), which is based on the synodic month, or time taken by the moon to make a complete circle around the Earth, had been invented at least 300 years before the Gregorian calendar, which is in effect a solar calendar, in Europe (Hashimoto, 2001).

Talking more about sciences, Liu Hui [刘徽] in his *Sea Island Manual* (海岛算经, c. 263) measured the sun's height by the lengths of a shadow cast on an upright rod. By comparing geographical distances and spaces, the Chinese employed their own mechanical, scientific methods that relied on empirical proofs devised by their ancestors, rather than axiomatic proofs preferred by the ancient Greeks and devised by their ancestors (Jami, 2001). As a rule, in traditional Chinese mathematics, a geometric problem was almost universally converted into an algebraic problem, quite different from the geometrical approach used in Euclid's *Elements*.

Surprisingly, today traditional Chinese mathematics like mechanical proofs or 'Wu Wenjun's method' are experiencing a revival in computational sciences, just as Chinese medicine, Chinese education, and Chinese politics are in their respective fields; all these disciplines are now striving again for recognition in world science.

To sum up, only after the West, culturally and scientifically, invaded the Eastern hemisphere, did mathematics in China become the universally axiomatic-deductive driven vehicle it is today. But Western invasion was not the precursor for sciences in China. Science had been in East Asia before, if only in a different, unique fashion (Needham, 1956; Jami, 2001).

Fortunately, in this century, the Western-fabricated fairy tale of former Eastern 'backwardness' and Western 'glory' has been dispelled. In reality, Eastern knowledge and Western knowledge are fairly balanced and complementary, and always have been.

As Francis Bacon and James Clerk Maxwell (1831-1879, mathematician and theoretical physicist) have sufficiently explained, ideally, the most sincere science is done today when *both* the inductive and the deductive methods find their due application. In some disciplines we prefer the inductive way, namely in the arts, while in many disciplines we tend to use both, like in sociology, archaeology, psychology, philosophy – the humanities. In others still we prefer the deductive way, like in mathematics, physics, biology, chemistry – the classical sciences. Yet ideally, induction and deduction should be used in a more balanced way.

Maxwell's equations are a good example of a successful synthesis: He carefully applied first the deductive method in proving several equations in seemingly separate fields of research, then the inductive method to demonstrate that electricity, magnetism, and even light are all manifestations of the same phenomenon: the electromagnetic field. It is like seeing each tree, and then the whole forest, but never both quite at the same time. This demonstrates an 'ideal' way of problem-solving by picking up a single successful case out of a million yet undecided ones.

A discovery of revolutionary proportions in the evolution of culture: An entire civilization, the East, goes down a more induction-based path, arriving at universals; while another civilization, the West, goes down the exact opposite, a more deduction-based path, arriving at particulars? If that is indeed what happened, it would constitute a discovery of great consequence: It would mean that 'superior' Western history has been ideologically and methodically biased, if not inherently flawed, throughout the ages:

> *The academic discipline of history is inevitably ideological in essence. Regardless of what might be the case with individual historical events, historical narration is always the result of a series of selective choices, so that the influence of the historian's standpoint is inescapable.*
> (Toshio Kuroda, 1990)

Universal history, as explained in this book, requires at least two points of view. As Joseph Needham (1951), Sir Geoffrey Ernest Richard Lloyd (1996), and Jonathan Spence (2001) – all three were married to Chinese women – demonstrated to Western audiences, China's contributions to humankind in traditional mathematics, medicine, statecraft, and agriculture had developed even before the First Qin Emperor's unification of China up to the Song (宋 960-1127-1279) and Yuan Dynasties (元 1271-1368) (Wu, 2007). In the course of just over one publication series, *Science and Civilization in China* (1954-2000), European scholars were up in arms at the sensational, if not horrifying news that Europeans owe their paper money, matches, umbrellas, playing cards, and whisky all to some blueprints of an unfamiliar Chinese mastermind (Temple, 2007). It comes as no surprise that the Chinese Communist Party and Chinese Ministry of Education readily adopted Needham's thesis that so more often than not eulogizes those good old days *When Asia Was the World* (Gordon, 2007).

In addition, and to the embarrassment of serious scholars, the 'History of Sciences in China' became the hobbyhorse for tens of thousands of amateur scholars, exchange students, tourists, and backpackers from around the world who tried to trace anything European or American back to its alleged Asian roots. Today, newspapers, computers, soccer, even German sauerkraut and sausages, Italian pasta and pizza, Reggae and Bob Marley have their firmly established Chinese progenitors (among the latter of whom are Vincent and Patricia Chin of Randy's Records in Jamaica, if you insist on knowing).

Yet, whatever this new wave of twenty-first century 'Eastern enlightenment of the West,' often mixed with institutionalized overstatement and euphemism in sensation-seeking media or some individuals' fancies – even the most frivolous ambition to remedy the past failures of Asia for the glory of her future cannot hide the fact, as the historians Joseph Needham, Catherine Jami, Peter Engelfriet, Geoffrey Lloyd, and

Li Tiangang described it, that China in particular had not developed or not sufficiently developed anything in the way of science and technology that could compete with the Western Imperialist's model, which in turn attested the Chinese were a people of 'arrested development' (Gu, 1922). I call the Western Imperialist's model "rather lucky than good," because some scholars, by bending history to the point of breaking, want us to believe that 'evil' Western dominance in Asia can only be explained by the lucky insensitivity of scientific discoveries like rifles and cannons (Chirot, 1991), surpassing the firecrackers made of China's gunpowder. Others, like Janet Abu-Lughod (1989) for example, point to the 'moment of China's political weakness' during the fall of the Mongols in the thirteenth century and coined the phrase 'bad luck for Asia,' which was "exploited by the Europeans who lacked any singularly innovative entrepreneurial scientific, or otherwise worthwhile advantages, except perhaps an exceptionally nasty tendency to conduct their large-scale trade as piracy" (Abu-Lughod, 1989).

Despite Western dominance, the Chinese 'civilization' (the correct name is wenming [文明]) had its advantages. The strong Confucian tradition of self-cultivation, learning, and memorization, with the translation and integration of foreign thoughts "for the purpose of understanding the West on Chinese terms" (Malhotra, 2011) reaching back to the early Buddhist monks during the Six Dynasties (222-589), has a remarkable consistency that ultimately proves a point:

It is important you should remember, that this nation of children, who live a life of the heart, [...] have yet the power of mind and rationality [...] which has enabled them to deal with the complex and difficult problems of social life, government and civilization with a success which, I will venture to say here, the ancient and modern nations of Europe have not been able to attain. (Gu Hongming, 1922)

I could go on, but before I do: It might strike some Europeans as outright offensive, but the truth is that they are not the only ones claiming the title of the fittest when it comes to 'surviving' history. To put it into historical perspective: The Chinese Empire was united in the year 221 BC under the Qin (秦) Emperor, some 1,997 years before Thomas Jefferson drafted the Declaration of Independence for the USA in 1776. India's sense of unity, ethnic diversity and, yes, democratic roots grew out of necessity because of her 'composite religious culture' some 2,500 years ago. By contrast, the Europeans today are struggling even with a constitutional treaty.

Two Incommensurable Realities

Discussing the East-West dichotomy in cultural terms became popular again in social science in the 80's and 90's, with the revival of the ideas of Ibn Khaldun (1332-1406), Auguste Comte (1798-1857), Emile Durkheim (1858-1917), and Arnold Toynbee (1889-1975). The goal of international scholarship was nothing less ambitious than to categorize all the world's cultures, to evaluate them, to dissect them, to discover and reveal patterns, and to make predictions about when they peak, when they struggle, and when they inevitably fall (Kennedy, 1987; CCTV, 2006).

The father of sociology, Ibn Khaldun, wrote:

The goal of civilization is sedentary culture and luxury. When civilization reaches that goal, it turns toward corruption and starts being senile, as happens in the natural life of living beings. (Ibn Khaldun, 1377)

Comparing cultures to living beings has been the scientific trend ever since Khaldun. In today's Western sociology, we now have plenty of exciting – if not incredible – choices (read: interpretations) of a culture's 'rise and fall':

- "youth, growth, maturation and decline" (Spengler, 1917) ;
- civilizations "taking turns or going in circles" (Ji, 2006);
- a "masculine West vs. a feminine East" (Garrison, 2000);
- nations "marrying and divorcing" each other (Griffiths, 1982);
- countries "collecting and redistributing credits for scientific discoveries" among them in a "Grand Titration" (Needham, 2004);
- an insurmountable "Great Divide" (Horton & Finnegan, 1973);
- either a "psychic unity" or a "secularization"

(Berger, 1966; 1974);
- a "de-secularization" (Berger, 1999);
- a "flat world" (Friedman, 1962; 1990; 2006);
- "globalization" or "many globalizations" (Berger & Huntington, 1974);
- brutal and straightforward "neo-Darwinism" (Heinsohn, 2003);
- plenty of "Empire" (Hardt & Negri, 2001), produced by one 'kind' of corporate man – preferably one of Aryan descent (Gellner, 1979).

This twentieth century "Cultural Heat" (Ji, 2006) that is reaping social theories by the bushel is well documented, and it is impossible to discuss them all.

What all theories have in common, however, and what has not changed in this new twenty-first century, as it has never been seriously challenged for the last two millennia, is a universe of facts from philosophy, politics, and now evolutionary biology, social and linguistic anthropology that seems to suggest that the history of civilization – and thus all human identity – is built on and around the *fundamental differences* and interaction among and between groups, populations, and cultures, and that the one difference and the one interaction that matter the most are those of the *two great cultural systems*: the *West* and its *Other*.

Perhaps the most striking phenomenon in cultural studies today is the revival of Max Weber's 'ideal types of cultures' that do facilitate progress and those that do not. Arnold Joseph Toynbee loved those cultural league tables, too. A new blame game was launched to find the latest 'sick-men-of-Europe,' the next 'youth bulge' (Goldstone, 1991; Fuller, 1995; Heinsohn, 2003), 'another failed (Arab) state,' a 'left behind,' an 'axis of evil,' an 'empire in decline,' the 'Chinese Century' (Shenkar, 2004), the 'New Asian Hemisphere' (Mahbubani, 2008), the 'yellow peril,' or just another victim for the 'War on Terror.'

Sensationalist literature about cultural comparison is abundant: In the West we have Samuel Huntington (1993; 2000; 2004), Francis Fukuyama (1992), Jared Diamond (2003; 2006), Milton Friedman (1962; 1990; 2006), Daniel A. Bell (2000; 2012), and Jürgen Habermas (1996; 2003; 2006). In the East we have Ji Xianlin [季羡林] (2006), Gu Zhengkun [辜正坤] (2003), Tu Weiming [杜维明] (2000; 2003), Kishore Mahbubani (2008), and Rajiv Malhotra (2011), to name but a few important contributors.

According to Max Weber (1864-1920), Western standards, institutions of law, science, education, and economics reflect Western analysis-based rationalism, and this may explain why the West got rich and technologically advanced before the East did (Weber, 2001). That underlying promise proved to be believable. Today, virtually every historical piece of scientific and economical evidence has been used against the Eastern people to demonstrate the – seemingly irrefutable – fact that the West was and (still) is the single most important and the only leading creative force of humankind. In fact, the only way for an Indian, Arab, or Chinese person to get some personal integrity in this world was to become Westernized, study at a Western university, or work for a Western international cooperation. The East, it seemed, was never in the position to ask for anything except for trouble.

Unfortunately, Max Weber could not read Japanese, Chinese, Hindi, Urdu, Arabic, Korean, Thai, or any other Eastern language. In fact, he who was arguably the world's greatest Orientalist had never been to the Orient. We could say then that he was a German rationalist at the time when Germany was an Imperial power (1871-1918). In those old days leading up to two devastating world wars, it was entirely sufficient for a German rationalist and "sociologist" (for that's what they call Max Weber) of his affluence to explain the mechanics of world history not by empirical investigation or observation, but – just like the other occasionally sinophobic Germans Immanuel Kant (1724-1804), Karl Wilhelm Friedrich Schlegel (1772-1829), Friedrich Wilhelm Joseph Schelling (1775-1854), Johann Gottfried Herder (1744-1803), and Georg Wilhelm Friedrich Hegel (1770-1831) before him – by miraculous, rational inquiry from the comfort of his study.

Few people realize that the Bible discourages people from studying foreign languages. The story of the Tower of Babel teaches us that there is one humanity (God's), but that "our languages are confused." From a historical European perspective, that has always meant that, say, any German philosopher could know exactly what the Chinese people were thinking, only that he couldn't understand them. So instead of learning the foreign language, he demanded a translation.

Coincidentally, or maybe not quite so, History with a capital 'H' followed the Bible. The first German philosopher, Gottfried Wilhclm Leibniz (1646-1716), *encouraged* his fellow Germans to do research on China, yet at the same time he warned against the use of foreign or 'un-Teutsch' [un-Germanic] words and concepts (Leibniz, 1677). This business of trying to understand China without taking the pains to study the Chinese language is well documented. When the German logician and first German 'China expert' Christian Wolff (1679-1754) got his hands on Latin translations by François Noël (1711) and Philippe Couplet (1687) of the Confucian Classics (Wolff was a Latin speaker), his reaction, I imagine, may have been something like this: He reads the *Lun Yu* in Latin and exclaims something like "Great, that looks very familiar; I have the feeling that I totally understand this Confucius!" (Wolff, 1721). Disturbing, isn't it?

Wolff was so confident about his newly-won knowledge about China that he went on to lecture about the Chinese as if he was *the* expert on all things China. Among his unforgettable findings were "Motiva Sinarum" ("The Motives of the Chinese"), "Summum bonum Sinarum" ("The Highest Good of the Chinese"), or "Finis Sinarum ultimus" ("The Final Purpose of the Chinese"), and so on (Wolff, 1721). And, of course, when somebody occasionally asked Master Wolff why he didn't visit China (to his defense, that was almost unthinkable in 1721), the greatest sinologist of all time dismissed the question with a wave of his hand by replying, "the wisdom of the Chinese was generally not so highly valued that it was necessary to travel there for its sake" (Albrecht, 1985).

Other historians followed in Wolff's footsteps. After all, why learn Chinese to become a pundit on China if Wolff took a shortcut? In fact, Wolff sufficiently demonstrated that just about any European could become a "China expert" without learning a single Chinese character.

This attitude prevailed regarding just about any foreign language. Now we know why the German philosopher Immanuel Kant could reasonably announce the "End of All Things" and Georg Hegel could proclaim the "End of History." Both learned men were very much aware that they had not mastered any non-European language in their lifetime, and they simply assumed that History was a bit like that, too.

This haughty attitude in the Western hemisphere has not changed; most Europeans still labor under the illusion that the Chinese "speak their languages," only that they "talk" in Chinese. Take the case of 'democracy' and 'human rights.' Those are terms that originated in Europe and do not have 1:1 equivalents in Chinese. Imagine China turned the tables and demanded that Europe apply more wenming (文明, civilization) and tian ren he yi (天人合一, oneness of heaven and man).

The European attitude is reflected in its translations. Most Westerners simply translate every key Chinese concept into convenient biblical or philosophical terminology. As a result, the Western image of China is literally Chinese-free.

For the same reason, in comparative cultural studies, if you had given Max Weber a fictional race, let's say the Smurfs, undoubtedly he would have produced a very elegant argument why the Smurfs never built a financial empire and got rich, as the Protestants in Europe so splendidly did, based on the simple and irrefutable fact that Smurfs are not Protestants. This, of course, is a tautology of epic proportions (e.g. Smurfs are Smurfs are no Protestants), and, consequently, a proposition true under any possible circumstance, while at the same time utterly useless for achieving true knowledge about the empirical world. For that reason, Max Weber's theory in sociology – like Sigmund Freud's in psychology or Karl Marx's in economics – has fallen out of favor. This is not so much because his work is inherently non-scientific, but more because his dialogue with other cultures is really a *self-serving, tedious monologue.*

Another, perhaps more elegant, explanation of Western historical dominance over world affairs was given by the late Edward Said (1935-2003), founder of 'post-colonial theory' in his masterpiece *Orientalism* (1978) and – independently – by Linda Hutcheon in *The Politics of Post-Modernism* (1989). Post-colonial theory essentially says that Orientalism, the study of Eastern cultures, religions, and languages, is the creation ('brain-child' is the fashionable term, I believe) of Western scholarship. Western scholars had written Asia's history through the lens of their Eurocentric world view, just like the Greeks did with the Persians, thereby only enhancing the exotic 'otherness' of the Eastern hemisphere. Said and Hutcheon argue that 'post-colonial' and then 'post-modernist' theories are both Western concepts. Moreover, they argue they are syntheses of the European Enlightenment's bourgeois rationalism as thesis on the one hand, and modernism as the antithesis on the other.

Bourgeois rationalism, modernism, and post-modernism could be categorized as the Age of Reason (seventeenth-eighteenth centuries), the Age of Totalities (nineteenth - beginning of the twentieth centuries), and the Age of Uncertainty (mid-twentieth century). As Said and Hutcheon would agree then, the East did not experience any of these categorizations, just as the West did not experience a Bolshevik

Revolution (1918), Communism (1918-1989), the Chinese Revolution (1926-1949), the Cultural Revolution (1966-1976), or the opening-up era under Deng Xiaoping (1979-1997).

I thereby conclude that neither hemisphere necessarily has to experience the other hemisphere's history in order to proceed with its own. There is a *philosophical misconception* in the writings of many Western scholars that seems to suggest that China and India will never catch up, because they only recently reached an early industrial age and missed out on the (Western) Enlightenment.

If the development of culture were, like most Western scholars would have it, essentially a one-way causal process like climbing a ladder, why did the Romans or Greeks on their way to becoming a proper civilization never produce Confucius, Mencius, the Tang Dynasty, the *Rgveda*, the *Brahmanas* or the *Mahabharata*? Surely, if we take the simple metaphor of history as a life-tree, similar to Ernst Haeckel's 'Tree of Life' (1897) in biology, in its earliest stage it could well have branched into two separate directions, with no subsequent coalescence possible (Haeckel, 2004). One branch could have developed into the Western hemisphere and represented history in a manner based on deduction, causality, and rationality. The other branch could have developed into the Eastern hemisphere and represented history in a manner based more on induction, interconnectedness, and universality. But it would still be 'one' history-tree, or maybe two different trees, albeit not too far apart. So, what makes so many Western sensationalists think that these trees or branches could possibly 'clash,' as in *The Clash of Civilizations* (Huntington, 1993)? Isn't it more reasonable to think that branches or sub-branches of history may die off, wither, break, become lost or forgotten rather than 'to clash'? Surely, if the militant West wishes a *clash* of civilizations, a *clash* it will be, albeit an uninspiring, unimaginative, and utterly senseless one. This because the Western hemisphere still does not wholly appreciate the grand alternative and worthy goal of engaging the East based on mutual respect and using an 'inclusive approach.' Instead, the West grafts Western branches on the Eastern tree by applying Western terminology to Eastern concepts. This way the entire tree of history shines as a product of Western scholarship. The question remains

> *[w]hether the telos which was inborn in European humanity at the birth of Greek philosophy [...] is merely one among many other civilizations and histories, or whether Greek*

humanity was not rather the first breakthrough to what is essential to humanity as such. (Edmund Husserl, 1970)

The receptive, integration-based East has learned to appreciate the Western branch of knowledge for its very different views on many things. Yet, in turn it has been exploited, colonized, and humiliated by the West:

This is the character of the Chinese people [...] to cherish the meanest opinion of themselves, and believe that they are born to drag the car of Imperial Power.
(Georg Hegel, 1821)

The crux of the whole question affecting the Powers of the Western nations in the Far East lies in the appreciation of the true inwardness of the Oriental mind.
(Alexis Krausse, 1900)

Isn't it important in any relationship that both sides learn from each other and respect each other? If not, Johann W. von Goethe had this warning for those who cared to listen:

The Philistine not only ignores all conditions of life which are not his own but he also demands that the rest of mankind should fashion its mode of existence after his own. (Estelle Morgan, 1958)

Regrettably, it is persistently this Philistine element in her soul that dominates Europe's actions. As a result, it is not unusual to meet a Western 'expert' in the streets of Shanghai or Beijing who has never heard of Si Maqian (司马迁), Xu Guangqi (徐光启), Lu Xun (鲁迅), Hu Shi (胡适), Ji Xianlin (季羡林), or Guo Morou (郭末若). Yet, if asked for his opinion on the Chinese language and culture, his chest will swell and, having himself mastered not more than a dozen Chinese characters, he will reply that his own failure in mastering those 65,000 Chinese ideographs begs the question of whether the ultimate cause of China's backwardness in the sciences is her very 'Chinese-ness' itself. China, Japan, India, and their neighbors are all seen as being at the receiving end of history; they receive *more* and (inherently) give *less* (Krausse, 1900; Husserl, 1970; Pyle, 2007).

Western nations seek a global civilization, which they believe is an *extension of their own*; while the Eastern nations, still cherishing their traditional cultures, will feel the 'rage of the

Western destabilizers' if they do not comply with Western aggression: "Chinese society bears a function of 'interior self-stability,' while the European society possesses an 'interiorly-installed unstable factor'" (Needham, 1964).

Accordingly, Western nations act as if they 'own' the globe, history, and all material objects. As soon as Asian nationals lay hands on any matters, material or any theories about matters or material, that very action is deemed a service to 'Westernization,' as if there was a Western patent on matter and modernity. There are Western tourists in Singapore, Shanghai, and Yokohama who genuinely believe that every house, bank, pair of high heels, traffic light, newspaper, computer, train, or automobile is a genuine extension of Western civilization.

Young Anglo-American visitors are especially quick to remind Asians that every English-language billboard marks Anglo-Saxon cultural territory. Few of them have learned in school that their own language is a relatively young branch of the Germanic language family, with those Germanic tribes, the Angles and the Saxons, being their immediate ancestors.

We may forgive those clueless, young Asia-bashers. But for the sake of dignity and cultural diversity, they should be properly educated that the chief end of Asian man is not to glorify the Anglo-American way of life, or any other Western model. A global language, exchange, and economy are good things, but 'globalization' as the mediator between East and West will not make East into West, nor West into East. Buddhism has not made China an India, and Capitalism has not made Japan an America. To annihilate 'cultural diversification,' accumulated in thousands of years or more, might not be as easy after all, not even in an American corporate dream. Isn't a 'common sensibility' preferable to all this American talk about global culture and values (Zhao, 2005)? How about 'All under Heaven' (天下, tianxia), 'humanity' (仁, ren), or 'harmonious society' (和谐社会, hexie shehui) – are those not more honest guarantors for mutual respect and dignity among civilizations?

An example of East and West talking at cross purposes would be the memorable conversation between Albert Einstein and Rabindranath Tagore on July 14, 1930. It shows, quite nicely I think, Einstein's limits to fully appreciate what Tagore wants to communicate, namely that the Western notion of causality has its limits. Consequently, Einstein quite diplomatically dismisses Eastern mysticism as unscientific and, implicitly, as rather unhelpful:

> Tagore: "I was discussing with Dr. Mendel today the new mathematical discoveries which tell us that in the realm of infinitesimal atoms chance has its play; the drama of existence is not absolutely predestined in character."
> Einstein: "The facts that make science tend toward this view do not say good-bye to causality."
> Tagore: "Maybe not, yet it appears that the idea of causality is not in the elements, but that some other force builds up with them an organized universe." [...]
> Einstein: "I believe that whatever we do or live for has its causality; it is good however, that we cannot see through it."
> (Rabindranath Tagore, 1931)

One can see from this "whatever" Einstein "cannot see through" that, in his Western view, it must be linear and causally related. Einstein *a priori* rules out – as it seems fit for any proper scientist – any alternative to Western-style causality. It also seems out of the question for Einstein and the culture he represents to think that there is any concept other than a scientific, rational Western one – let alone that of an 'ancient

Oriental wizard' (Kawabata, 1969). Rudyard Kipling's poem "East is East, and West is West, and never the two shall meet" easily comes to mind (Kipling, 1999).

What would have happened if Tagore had brought up the continuum of 'samsara,' 'non-violence,' 'free will,' 'karma,' the function of impermanent, unsatisfactory, empty, and lacking-a-self 'dharmas,' or just 'good poetry'? Surely, there must be more wisdom than Western science in this world:

Perhaps in return for conquest, arrogance and spoliation, India will teach us the tolerance and gentleness of the mature mind, the quiet content of the unacquisitive soul, the calm of the understanding spirit, and a unifying, a pacifying love for all living things. (Will Durant, 1930)

Land of religions, cradle of the human race, birthplace of human speech, grandmother of legend, great grandmother of tradition. The land that all men desire to see and having seen once even by a glimpse, would not give that glimpse for the shows of the rest of the globe combined. (Mark Twain, 1897)

In my understanding, the two global hemispheres experienced different, unique histories, and this made them what they are today. What did the existentialists teach us about identity? Isn't it the case that the beginning of human history determined what we are, but our historical experience determines *who* we are? Shouldn't we all agree that we are a – more or less identical – human race? However, thousands of years of unique history have made us *who* we are: Chinese, Indians, Japanese, Germans, French, British etc., and, eventually, we shaped the East and the West.

I will not attach importance to every cultural leaf or twig and say that any particular culture should be preserved, nor will I harbor the illusion that everything can be preserved. Having said this, however, the smallest leaves and twigs will bend and break when the weather becomes harsh, and wither when the tree is not well nurtured. If our criterion was 'longevity,' however, we would be safest to bet on the two great cultural systems: the East and the West.

To conclude, the argument that East and West look at history from different angles is to be refuted: History is local, and lends itself to different points of view. We have every reason to believe that the two hemispheres not only look at and interpret history differently, but irreversibly *experience* their very own local version of it. In addition to experience, the different cognitive preferences of the Easterner and Westerner inevitably let them, in a metaphysical sense, *prefer* their own version of history and *misinterpret* the other's. This predicament, I believe, is impossible to overcome because Easterners and Westerners cannot experience each other's histories nor see them through the same eyes. The East perceives history to be more holistic and interconnected, while the West regards history as more linear and fragmented.

The Theory of Power
and to Whom It Belongs

Western analytical-based societies, with their emphasis on achieving 'useful' knowledge, became masters of nature, with the perspective of active domination over other civilizations.

While in the integration-based societies knowledge came from studying the classics, the wise, and the kings of old, the analysis-based West started to categorize and deconstruct nature and all things. Periodism, for example, is characteristically related to Western rationalism, as opposed to non-event related dynasties named after Chinese emperors, so is categorization as a method to acquire new knowledge *ad infinitum*. Western societies dress themselves in the mantle of knowledge, and knowledge is linked to power, which has been the very source of European predominance:

> *We should admit [...] that power produces knowledge [...] that power and knowledge directly imply one another [...] that there is no power relation without the correlative constitution of a field of knowledge.*
> (Michel Foucault, 1977)

The concept of power in the integration-based East, however, is sheer might in numbers, uniformity, and thus consistency. This spiritual 'moral power' drove out the Imperialists in the first half of the twentieth century:

> *The truest test of civilization, culture and dignity is character, not clothing.* (Mahatma Gandhi, 1938)

To sum up, Western power in my taxonomy is related to analytically-based deductive knowledge, whereas Eastern power is related to integration-based inductive knowledge. The former has the historical function of a dangerous, yet creative force; the latter has the historical function of a tranquil, yet moral force.

The Problem of Standard

Qian Binsi [钱宾四] wrote in his *Chinese Intellectual History* (*Zhongguo Sixiang Shi,* 中国思想史(1991):

"中国文化过去最伟大的贡献，在于对'天''人'关系的研究." *If you cannot read what I just wrote, that means you probably don't understand Chinese. It says: "Among all those past contributions of Chinese culture (to mankind), the study of the relation between 'heaven' and 'man' is the grandest"* (Qian Binsi, 1998).

Without knowing Chinese, it is, I would argue, very difficult to understand Chinese people. Sadly, not knowing Chinese is the rule among Western commentators on the East-West discourse: from the political thinkers Charles de Montesquieu (1689-1755) and Jeremy Bentham (1748-1832), over the great writers Denis Diderot (1713-1784) and Johann Wolfgang von Goethe (1749-1832), the economist and moral philosopher Adam Smith (1723-1790), to the anthropologist Claude Lévi-Strauss (1908-) and the three great 'fordmakers' in cultural studies: who? (1561-1626, he initiated the scientific revolution), Max Weber (1864-1920, the founder of the modern study of sociology), and Karl Marx (1818-1883, the father of Communism and dialectic materialism). Similarly, in philosophy we have the highly gifted Gottfried Leibniz (1646-1716), Friedrich Wilhelm Joseph Schelling (1775-1854), Georg Wilhelm Friedrich Hegel (1770-1831), Jacques Derrida (1930-2004), Arthur Schopenhauer (1788-1860), and Bertrand Russell (1872-1970). All of them wrote passionately about the Confucian and/or Buddhist canon, categorized the world's people, and judged their cultural outlook and *modus operandi*.

Now, of all the persons listed above, to my knowledge none of them had ever mastered Classical Chinese or Sanskrit, nor had learned any other Asiatic language.

But then, why should they? The *standard* of Western knowledge is Western civilization and, recently, it has become the English language, and against *that* standard all other cultures are measured and judged. Western man, not man, it seems, is the measure of all things:

> *There is something unique here in Europe that is recognized in us by all other human groups, too, something that [...] becomes a motive for them to Europeanize themselves even in their unbroken will to spiritual self-preservation, whereas we, if we understand ourselves properly, would never Indianize ourselves, for example.* (Edmund Husserl, 1935)

> *It is clear to all Chinese that Western culture is the root of wealth, success, development and political survival – it is the essence of modernity.* (Francesco Sisci, 2008)

This air of condescension is reflected in Western education systems. It is still perfectly conceivable to meet a German, French, Italian, or American visiting scholar on the streets of Delhi or Shanghai who has never heard of Rammohan Roy, Sri Autobindo, Ramakrishna Paramahansa, Si Maqian, Hu Shi, Liang Qichao, or Lu Xun. Outside Asia the situation is truly hopeless, with the average American Joe or European Karl not being able to name a single living Chinese person.

The histories of China, Japan, and India were not even mentioned before 2008 in the syllabus of Germany's compulsory secondary school curriculum. This ignorance of general (Asian) knowledge extends to grand literary works such as *Journey to the West*, *Outlaws of the Marsh*, the *Puranas*, or the *Ramayana*.

Even to this day, nine out of ten university professors of Chinese or Sanskrit/Hindi Studies in Europe are not able to write or communicate fluently in those languages, let alone to a level worthy of the highest intellectual standard. Most have to employ Chinese or Indian translators or assistants to help their 'white masters' carefully dissect those foreign texts as if they were insects on a piece of cardboard.

Are Europeans really that ignorant? Of course not. Far from it. In fact, they are really busy in all intellectual departments in keeping what they have, and maybe learning a bit more about finance, information technology, American pop culture, and the other 27 European Union member states. What they don't have are the spare time and human resources to master Eastern cultures and languages.

Only so much time and energy can be devoted to the pursuit of knowledge of other cultures without other aspects of our own culture suffering. In 1964, Germany proudly produced 1,357,000 children; but in the year 2006, the number shrank to 676,000 – out of which close to 30 percent were of non-German nationality (destasis, 2006). Therefore, it will be an impossible task for Germany to maintain its own culture, let alone learn a lot more new things. Take the Swedish nation as an example, a people of merely 8 million (of whom 20 percent are foreigners, but this aside). In order to preserve Swedish history and knowledge, China could send a mere 0.5 percent of its population to do the job. On the other hand, if the entire Swedish population tried to preserve Chinese history and knowledge, they would not only discontinue the Swedish cause, but would also venture no further than to preserve a tiny 0.5 percent of the Chinese tradition. It is therefore self-evident which countries have a greater capacity for cultural preservation.

Of all the cultures that have disappeared from this world, to my knowledge, not a single farewell letter or suicide note has ever been unearthed. It must be a painless, gradual, almost unnoticed just process. Some of the Goths, the East Germanic tribes who disappeared slowly after the sixth century, must have felt that their cities had too many foreigners, that their daughters preferred to marry outsiders, that their sons had to learn a foreign language, that they consumed more and more goods that they themselves did not produce, so that their few survivors suddenly felt the desire to belong to something greater than their own narrow turf.

In this twenty-first century of voyeurism and mass media though, we may want to hear and watch some cultures die. In drawing an analogy to Elisabeth Kübler-Ross's celebrated 'five stages of grief' (1969) – denial, anger, bargaining, depression, acceptance – certain European nations could be considered no longer in 'denial' but are already experiencing the next stage of their looming exodus, that of 'anger.'

Contrary to the Confucian laws of good manners or Indian tolerance and gentleness, Western media, especially the German, French, and British ones – in the name of the European monopoly on freedom, democracy, and human rights – leave out no opportunity to relentlessly and shamelessly lecture China on human rights, degrade Islam, satirize India, demonize the Persians (Iran), and mock all Russian ambitions – whatever floats the European boat.

I have not seen this helplessness and simultaneous finger-pointing in India, China, or the USA lately. On the contrary, these great and promising powers are optimistic and ambitious about their future. This was especially true in 2008 during the Olympic Games in Beijing that commanded the world's attention: "更高, 更快, 更强" ("Higher, faster, stronger," the Olympic motto). Chinese *aiguo zhuyi* [爱国主义] or "patriotism" has taken up the world stage. Since 1978, when Deng Xiaoping (1904-1997) proudly announced, "To get rich is glorious!" China experienced a 30-year period of unprecedented growth of national wealth and power, averaging 10 percent annual GDP growth. This sudden increase of wealth in such a short period of time is considered unprecedented in the history of humankind, and it didn't happen in the West (Khanna, 2008; Kim, 2006): "They undergo compulsory Maoism courses but fantasize of little but money" (Aiyar, 2008). The Chinese love their country, and they embrace life. They also have many serious problems. They know it, but they would – as all great powers do – rather continue to be great and engage with other great nations, and not waste too much time with the negative, nagging, and left-behind former great nations, and certainly not with some jealous – but politically irrelevant – European demagogues.

The European nation states' diminishing roles in world politics, their declining populations (Heinsohn, 2004), the brain drain (*timeEurope*, 2004/01), and their reluctance to learn from other cultures (Phelps, 2007) are all irreversible and accelerate year by year. Even the hope for a suffering in fragmentary unity – I am talking about the hope for a 'United States of Europe' (Reid, 2004) – proved short-sighted when a European constitution was first ruled out, and finally a European Treaty was rejected twice in 2005 by France and The Netherlands, and in 2008 by Ireland. Furthermore, in case of a referendum in Great Britain, 89 percent of the British public would fervently vote against the 'damn Treaty' (BBC, 2008/02). A great piece of advice will be needed to steer the European boat through these difficult times. I have one from Buddhism: "Not to live in living is to endure. Not to die in dying is to live on" (Kumarajiva, 2008).

What then is the true problem with Europe? Why don't the European nations unite and become 'one'? I will argue that in the past 2,500 years of its history, there has never been the concept of 'oneness' or 'harmoniousness' in the European collective mind. The powerful poet Johann W. von Goethe said: "There are two peaceful powers in this world: *Right* and *Tact*" (Goethe, 1833). And Gu Hongming observed, "希伯来人的文明

宗教教导欧洲人正义的知识，但没有教导礼法" ("The Religion in the civilization of the Hebrew people taught the people in Europe the knowledge of Right, but it did not teach Tact") (Gu, 1922). The Greeks knew about *Tact* and taught the Romans. The Romans tried to teach the Germanic tribes *Tact* and *Right*, but the Germanic tribes could only understand *Right*, not *Tact*. Thus, the emperors of the Holy Roman Empire (962-1806), from the King of the Franks Charlemagne (747-814) to Francis II (1768-1835), later Emperor of Austria, did not know how to rule *tactfully*, and their subjects did not know how to submit *tactfully*. About that same Empire, the French Enlightenment philosopher Francois Voltaire remarked that "it was neither holy, nor Roman, nor an empire." For a start, despite its name, it never did include Rome. Then, observe in all those divided territories, there were quarreling tribes and countless families that "live[d] scattered and apart, surrounding their dwellings with open space" (Tacitus, 1996) – the Franks, the Dutch, the Swiss, today's Czech, Flemish, and Polish with no unifying *lingua franca*, opposing Prussia and Austria as well as the Church. It was a total mess. And what did the righteous Napoleon do? He did what he knew was *Right*: He steamrolled them again, thereby diffusing and dividing the already fragmented peoples; but he did not know how to unite, rule, or teach them *Tact* either.

The Chinese, on the other hand, knew only little about *Right*, but a lot more about *Tact*. Lao Zi said:

> 故大邦以下小邦，则取小邦；小邦以下大邦，则取大邦。故或下以取，或下而取。大邦不过欲兼畜人，小邦不过欲入事人。夫两者各得所欲，大者宜为下。
>
> *When a large country submits to a small country, it will adopt the small country. When a small country submits to a large country, it will be adopted by the large country. The one submits and adopts, the other submits and is adopted. It is in the interest of a large country to unite and gain service, and in the interest of a small country to unite and gain patronage. If both would serve their interests, both must submit.* (Lao Zi, 61).

Thus, there is a tactful bond between the small states imitating the large: *Submission is a means of union*. If you ask any of the fragmented 27 nation states of Europe today about their European Union, each of them would be quick to defend their individual *Right*, but none of them would have *Tact* enough to submit to the greater cause.

The 'fragmentary view' on the world enjoys the greatest prominence in the deductive West, namely in the categorization of the people of the world and their regions, followed by a rigorous system of classification (Sen, 2006). In other words, the Europeans want a similar fragmented Asia. Tibet is classified as Tibet, and its people as Tibetan, not as part of China and as Chinese (*Economist*, 2007/02). The unifying one-party political systems of Russia, Vietnam, Thailand, Myanmar, Iran, and China, or any other large concentration of power, offer outrageous non-European conditions. These are utterly revolting to the analytical Western intellect, and present a security risk to Western hegemony (Barnett, 2004) and the Western watchword of *divide et impera*.

With regard to China, Japan, Korea, Thailand, Vietnam and other such nations, the mere thought of 'Asian values,' their archaic forms of politeness, filial piety, spoiled 'little emperors,' submissive doll-like women, shyness in adult men, rote-learning, collectivism, tendency for authoritarian rule etc. – all these elicit a specific revulsion in the Western psyche. This revulsion is so pervasive and ongoing that I do not dare think of the irreversible and dangerous course of history that is looming over Asian civilization in case Europe and America cannot find themselves at peace with the new, Asiacentric world order. During the Cold War, the socialist Guy Mollet (1905-1975) is believed to have said, "The communists are not of the left but of the East."

That statement deserves its own branch of scholarship. First of all, it is based on facts. Far into the 70's, no communist party in Western Europe or the USA held any considerable mandates. Apart from France, Italy, and Finland, Communism was virtually absent in Western politics, except, of course, as the bogeyman. I cannot discuss the reasons here why collectivism, authoritarian rule, the spiritualization of materialism, socialism, and totalitarian concepts so easily caught on in the East, and why Joseph Stalin, Mao Zedong, Kim Jong-Il, and, yes, Adolf Hitler too, are still, despite acknowledged flaws, considered 'great leaders' among many Asian intellectuals and admirers. They will probably always be. Yet what I will discuss is how history is now repeating itself, after humankind has learned how dichotomy works.

The labeling that took place in Western Europe with regard to Communism as an ugly Eastern proposition is now taking place in Western Europe and the USA with regard to *harmoniousness*. Let us modify Guy Mollet's alleged statement about the communist and say: "The harmonizers are not of the liberals, but of the East."

I will explain this in a minute. Before, let us see what Amartya Kumar Sen, the Nobel Laureate in economics, had to say about the two civilization modes and their distinct views and approaches towards history:

> *There are two ways of thinking of the history of civilization in the world. One is to pursue the story in an inclusive form, paying attention to the divisions as well as the interdependence involved, possibly varying over time, between the manifestations of civilization in different parts of the world. This I shall call the 'inclusive approach.' The other, which I shall call the 'fragmentary approach,' segregates the beliefs and practices of different regions separately, paying attention to the interdependences between them as an afterthought (when any attention is paid to them at all).* (Amartya Kumar Sen, 2006)

The two ways of thinking in the history of civilization are reflected in humankind's approach towards 'Communism' and, in this age, towards 'harmoniousness.' The East is pursuing the story in the inclusive form of a multiverse; the West brutally segregates the beliefs of different regions. The West does not identify itself with the 'inclusive approach' and is now expelling the harmonizers, just like it expelled the communists before, from world history. Once the rigidity of the Western 'fragmentary approach' has been studied and understood, the hopelessness of any non-Western attempt to *get back into* world history will become apparent.

Indeed, after all the recent preemptive strikes on terrorists and failed states, the irreversible process of 'Westernization' and 'globalization,' the tiresome break with each and every civic code of mutual respect and non-interference in any nation's internal affairs, and the desire to conquer nature and, if necessary, the traditional peoples and tribes that made a pact with nature – how can we not say that the deductive West is completely rejecting the inductive Eastern notion of 'harmoniousness'?

Of course, with statements like "the West is rejecting 'harmoniousness'" it seems we are oversimplifying things again. Yet, like with all abstracts that seem simple, they are actually very complex: If we study the histories of the inductive East and the deductive West, and if we understand that the one went down the integration-based path while the other took the analysis-based path, we will come to understand that 'harmoniousness,' just like any other mental concept such as 'democracy,' must be understood in the respective Western context or in the respective Eastern context.

The abstract concepts of 'harmoniousness' or 'democracy,' for example, behave non-relative precisely in their respective Western or Eastern context where, of course, they may have other names and additional meanings, but will almost inevitably behave relative in any dialogue between the cultures. Here I will give an example of the so-called 'Golden Rule' in ethics, also called the 'Ethic of Reciprocity,' which is supposedly the origin of the Western position on human rights. In the Gospel of Luke 6;27-31, Jesus Christ said: "Do for others just what you want them to do for you. If you really do that, you may just find that your enemy will become your friend." I think this Golden Rule from the Bible is clear: In your own best interest, make your enemies friends. But what happens when you apply this to friends – will they become enemies?

Another often used application of the biblical Golden Rule is to warn someone about the pain and punishment that comes from breaking the Golden Rule, because once you break it, you cannot rule out that someone else is breaking it with regard to you. After all, who wants to be accused, beaten, and crucified? Despite the individualistic, very moving, and almost selfish touch of the biblical Golden Rule, it is among the best examples of 'harmoniousness' in the respective Western context. Moreover, according to its moral implications, all Western nations have encouraged their societies to promote the development of individuality by laws and variable decrees of punishment that will ensure your systematical punishment if another individual was harmed by you or your actions. This could be called the Western 'fragmentary approach' to the Golden Rule.

Now we will look at the Eastern 'inclusive approach' to the Golden Rule. Master Confucius formulated his Doctrine of Reciprocity roughly 500 years before Jesus Christ did: "己所不欲，勿施于人，在邦无怨，在家无怨" ("Do not do to others what you would not like yourself. In the state there will be no complaints, in the family there will be no complaints") (Confucius, *Lun Yu*, 12; 2). This Golden Rule of Confucius is at the core of 'harmoniousness' in the East, and according to its moral implications, all East Asian nations have encouraged their societies to promote the cultivation of oneself as an integrated member of the collective with various decrees of obedience and filial piety that will ensure shame and loss of 'face' [面子, mianzi] if the collective is harmed.

Few people in China fear punishment by law for one's misbehavior. What is feared most is 'loss of face', the 'feedback from the collective,' the 'wrath of one's family,' one's 'father's judgment,' and, yes, sometimes the Communist Party official's patronizing, often infantilizing propaganda: "This disgraceful bad citizen now prefers to feel ashamed." When one of the disciples of Confucius, Zi Gong [子贡], asked the Master: "Is there one word that can serve as a principle of conduct for life?," Confucius replied: "It is the word *shu* (恕) – reciprocity" (Confucius, *Lun Yu*, 15;23).

As an interim result, let us say that this simple Golden Rule "Do not unto others what you do not like yourself" is enforced in the West by laws and punishment, and in the East by morals and a sense of shame:

道之以政，齐之以刑，民免而无耻，道之以德，齐之以礼，有耻且格。

If the people are governed by laws, and punishment is used to maintain order, they will try to avoid the punishment but have no sense of shame.

If they are governed by virtue, and rules of propriety [ritual] are used to maintain order, they will have a sense of shame and will become good as well.

(Confucius, *Lun Yu*, 2;3)

Next, let us say that neither Jesus Christ nor Confucius is the voice or medium of an almighty God, but that their message was intended to become part of the universal code of ethics. What difference would it make? We would still have to read the Bible or *The Analects* to make sense of the real world. The human mind needs context. That is the bottom line. In the Western context 'harmoniousness' is defined by the Judeo-Christian tradition, while in the Sinitic context 'harmoniousness' is defined by the Confucian tradition. This is an example of what I meant by understanding harmoniousness in the respective Western context and in the respective Eastern context.

A people's history, value system, code of conduct, choices and priorities, family and spiritual life should always be seen and understood in that people's socio-cultural context. Most scholars of the cultural sciences and the arts and humanities know this very well. They accept the tremendous cultural diversity of our species, and thus almost as a humanistic reflex propose and prefer a dialogue among cultures and civilizations as a means to exchange ideas and opinions without forcing the other party to accept one's point of view (United Nations, 2001). But does it work?

As I said before with regards to communist theory, although to a large extent 'made in the West' by the seemingly singular effort of two men, Karl Marx and Friedrich Engels, the entire idea of Communism was almost immediately rejected by Western Europe simply because the context, the West's cultural mode and fragmentary approach, wasn't suited for it. On the other hand, the Eastern context, its cultural mode and inclusive approach, was suited for it, and considerable cultural and political will, time, and energy were spent to experiment and develop communist theories further. Isn't that remarkable? If you tell someone to "do it!" (the communist revolution), he won't do it. This happened in Europe with Karl Marx's ideas, which were considered utopian and dangerous. Conversely, if you really want someone to do it, you had better say "don't do it!" So much for Europe's warning about the dangers of Communism in Asia. Doesn't this explain why philosophical systems never last and religions last forever? All religions effectively say *don't*: Don't kill, don't lie, don't steal, don't commit adultery, and so on. But of course we do it all the time, so we deeply respect religion for its profound universal wisdom. The same holds true for the most accomplished spiritual leaders and the greatest of all sages. They often say something in the end like "Oh, but I really *don't know* anything," or "This is *not* at all my invention" – like Socrates and Confucius did – because precisely such a confession of one's own shortcomings will produce the exact opposite effect in the listener by arousing his sympathy: "Oh, sure he does!"

Likewise, the two great cultural systems of East and West will (almost) always try to sabotage each other's opportune ideas and ideologies, compromise hopes, destroy dreams, and say – for the sake of humanity – "I want to distinguish myself from you, no matter what it takes." There is a common African wisdom called "ubuntu," which roughly means "I am because you are." In intercultural relations and diplomacy it could also mean "I will not be you, but me, because of you." Let's recall the Golden Rule: Wouldn't it be, psychologically speaking, more honest to say "Do unto others; then they won't do it unto you." I am saying it because *this* (and *not* what the holy scripture recommends) is the reality practiced every day in world politics, economics, academia, law, and all human relations: It's about who dominates – and the damn law of human relationships. The biblical Golden Rule, Confucian reciprocity, and any similar concepts only work in their respective cultural context, and not abroad. Abroad, they are called cultural imperialism.

The West, despite all its condescension and sympathy for Asian ideas, is fundamentally rejecting the Asian 'inclusive approach' right in front of our eyes. The more Asia promotes her views on the so-called universality of 'oneness,' 'balance,' 'harmony,' 'integration,' or 'one commonwealth under tianxia,' the more Asia's theories become hers, and hers alone. The West will not waste its energies on anything that is inner-world dependent and all-inclusive; only that what the West discovered upon breaking that 'all-inclusive something' into its parts will make sense to the Western mind. This is the consequence of the deductive Western 'fragmentary approach' towards nature and all things.

Not that the USA or European nations do not have their own ideas about harmoniousness. Far from it: They have various, often fragmentary, even conflicting ideas about it. They always have. After the 'ejection' of Communism from the Western hemisphere, in the case of dialectical materialism, all major parties of Western capitalist democracies quickly found their own ways to satisfy the people and to curb production and the accumulation of material wealth, and it all happened without turning human beings into submissive production units with no human rights. Today, Germany and France are arguably more socialist than socialist China ever will be.

In the case of universal 'harmoniousness,' the major parties in deductive Western democracies have already found their own ways to cater to the people's need for ever more 'international flights,' 'foreign currencies,' 'world trade,' 'exchange,' 'cooperation,' and 'tolerance.' This is where the Western terms 'globalism,' 'multiculturalism,' 'cultural diversity,' 'democracy,' 'human rights' etc., all come in handy; no Asian alternative needed.

As a consequence, in a Western-dominated world no one could care less that "equilibrium is the great foundation of the world, and harmony is its path" (Zi Si & Zhong Yong, 1) and that "the function of rites (*li*) lies in harmoniousness" (Confucius, *Lun Yu* 1;12), or "to live with a culture is to understand that culture" (Lao Zi, 54). It is indeed very difficult to conceive that today's leaders of the free world – Barack Obama of the USA,

Francois Hollande of France, David Cameron of Great Britain, Angela Merkel of Germany, and so on – would favor 'oneness' over 'Westernization,' not to mention the Chinese dream of 'tianxia' (天下, All under Heaven). Again, this is the bottom line. There is no need for China's obsolete sense of tolerance, kindness, and gracefulness, Japan's 'universal emptiness,' the ancient Indian sense of 'universal equality,' 'universal tolerance,' or indeed any other spiritual ideal, no matter how many hundreds of years those great Eastern sages spoke prior to Jesus Christ, Bill Gates, or Harry Potter.

Billions of Asian hearts will have puffed with pride upon hearing that their countries were joining the United Nations, the World Trade Organization, or could attend yet another international conference, all in the name of 'globalism' that so much resembles, it seems, the eternal Eastern pursuit of interconnectness, oneness, balance, and harmoniousness as well as the Eastern need for 'self-cultivation' that has been the foundation of all traditional Eastern societies from the beginning of time. But are they getting more than they bargained for by joining a Western world order? The material benefits of submitting to the West are obvious: Western science, technology transfer, and materialism indeed look like freebies. How wonderful if the West also came over to your tent and acknowledged *your* cultural values, beliefs, and *your* ideas in exchange, no? But therein lies the rub: Except for a small circle of experts, hardly any educated Westerner has ever heard of the following stories of tolerance, which originated in the East, as for example in the *Book of History* (书经, c. 600 BC-300 BC) or the *Tipitaka* (also known as the *Pali Canon*, c. 500 BC-400 BC). Nor have many Westerners heard of the great hero Fu Xi (伏羲, legendary ruler and fordmaker of the *Book of Changes* or *I Ching* [易经] in 2800-2737 BC), or the Hindu/Jain traditions of 'Anekantavada' (meaning 'non-one-endedness,' a philosophy of universal tolerance), 'Syadvada' (a philosophical tradition of subjectivity and relativity in discourses), and so on.

So, I ask: How can someone appreciate someone else's cultural values if he does not know their content, language, or their origin? The answer is no one can; the West refuses to appreciate Eastern spirituality and its ways. A good example is that of "religion." Religion is a European word and concept. Therefore, there is only one religion. In fact, we are all living in it. We are all living in the year 2012 of our Lord, Jesus Christ. This so-called freedom of religion in Europe should be read and understood as "as long as we live on Christianity's terms, you may believe in whatever you want." Imagine Europe's reaction if we were to introduce the Chinese taxonomy of *jia, jiao,* and *xue* (meaning schools, teachings, and learning). Then there wouldn't be any "religion" at all. Even "philosophy," instead of being the global Western syndicate it is today, would be reduced to this: a tiny Hellenic branch of Plato's *jia.*

Was it not Thomas Kuhn, the great American scientist, who said that "rival paradigms are incommensurable" (Kuhn, 1970)? Incommensurability means that although it is always possible to imitate each other, it is almost impossible to understand, for example, a Chinese paradigm through let us say the conceptual framework and biases of the European looking glass, and vice versa. Of course, the inductive East and the deductive West keep trying: "Now that thirty million Chinese study piano and another ten million study violin, Western classical music well may have become the dominant form of transcendental experience for Asians even while Western neuroscientists dabble in what they think is Buddhism" (*aTimes*, 2008/07).

What is *in* that shiny pot for us at the long end of the rainbow called globalization? I am not talking about material wealth but about spiritual enlightenment. It appears that the integration-based Eastern traditions search for oneness and harmoniousness, for final confirmation that they also belong to this world, in the same pot in which the Western traditions know they will find a substance that reflects their own image. What can be done, if anything, about these completely different attitudes towards knowledge to avoid global misunderstandings?

The psychological conundrum for Asia is that due to its induction-based views on the world, it does not perceive those European countries as isolated and self-sufficient, but rather as an integrated and dependent part of humankind. Thus, because Asia always strives for universal tolerance and harmony, it readily believes Western views or at least will always consider them as part of the solution.

The West, however, is different. Apart from a few premises that it chooses to work with at any specific moment, the West usually does not consider other countries' noises and fusses. It does not take into account all the facts, the history, the respective Eastern context, the whole picture, but isolates a few propositions each time and draws its conclusions accordingly. Its deductive method is precise and sharp as a surgeon's knife. When the official spokesman for ZDF ('Second German Television,' a German television broadcaster) came to Shanghai in 2008 and held a talk on journalism governed by public law, he embarrassed the Tongji University of Shanghai, and, I believe, many more people than just his host, by laying down some abstract German premises about 'freedom of the press' and 'human rights.' You see, there are thousands of German expatriates, consultants, and students in Shanghai impatiently waiting for the day when China will do as the Germans want them to do. The television spokesman drew his conclusion about what any *rational* man, as opposed to a non-rational Chinaman, I suppose, would consider 'good journalism,' following a point-by-point deductive-style hell of an argument. In short, he acted like a surgeon transplanting a liver. You cannot use Chinese chopsticks to transplant a liver, you see. There can be no mistake about what a liver is. And about where it is. All the parameters are highly scientific and precise. We know what a good operation looks like, and we know what follows if all the premises are true: The patient walks out of the hospital. When a Chinese professor in broken German informed the audience firstly that reality was more complex and that the Chinese position also had to be taken into account, and secondly that German media coverage of Tibet and other politically sensitive topics was biased and often untrue, and that German media evidently even used Nazi-German terminology such as 'Jubelchinesen' for Chinese volunteers who simulated spontaneous joy and cheerfulness during the Beijing Olympic Games torch relay, the German lecturer replied in disbelief: "Nun seien Sie mal nicht so weinerlich!" meaning "Come on, don't be such a whiner!"

A Loveless Darwinian Desert

The great scientists Thomas S. Kuhn (1922-1996) and Karl Popper (1902-1994), the venerable Scottish essayist Thomas Carlyle (1795-1881), and the great historian Joseph Needham (1900-1995) all concluded that the evolution of science is *non-relativistic*, which tells us that the deduction-based West was more or less *predestined* to pick up the scientific way.

No matter what those few smart Eastern individuals invented – be it the compass in the second millennium before the birth of Jesus Christ; the so-called 'South-pointing carriage' of the Duke of Zhou of the Zhou Dynasty, also in the second millennium before our Lord, and a forerunner of the 'magnetic compass' which was finally invented in China about a decade before the Three Wise Men visited Jesus after his birth, obviously without a compass (they used the stars); the so-called 'South-pointing ladles;' the magnet; the kite; the astronomical clock; the pizza; the noodle; or even gunpowder – it all does not lead to greatness in the sciences if one's society is a victim of its own inward-looking traditions.

Once these Asian inventions 'popped up' in the West, the European nations took their chances, developed the sciences, increased industrial output, perfected weaponry, boiled the noodle, and set out to conquer and divide the globe among themselves. Only *afterwards* did the West invent patents, copyrights, laws, and ideas about intellectual property to ensure it would forever stay in power, could forever keep what it took, cunningly assuming that – as I explained before – evolution, even the evolution of sciences and culture, is but a gradual, developmental progress, like, say, climbing a ladder, and whoever takes the first step owns it to the last.

For obvious reasons, the Western 'scientific accomplishments' of the past still confuse many Asians, who, as I said elsewhere, excel in so many arts, crafts, and the humanities, but – more importantly – outnumber the Europeans today by roughly six to one. In a 'democratic' world order, Asian opinions would clearly outweigh European ones. With her sheer numbers, China in particular would win any poll against angry Germany, France, and Great Britain: "Hey, you Europeans, you want a 'world democracy' and 'global equality'? Well, here you are! Where do we vote?"

Would it be wrong, in a democratic world order, to drastically reduce the global influence of Europe's 'Great Three' in terms of political, economic, and voting power to 1.28, 0.84, and 0.81 respectively, according to their share of the world's population? I think so, because I grew up in a democratic system. Yet, this is not going to happen. Not in the United Nations, not in Europe. The European mind got itself absolutely accustomed to the idea that it constitutes the world's 'bourgeoisie' or 'global elite,' the gem among stones, while the developing world is human soup. It has no *Tact*, thus no respect for the rest, and it will never know its proper place. Western, seemingly universal ideas of 'democracy' and 'equality' stop at their own garden's fences. Beyond that lies a vast and loveless *Darwinian desert*.

As someone once wisely observed (Lao Zi, if you must know), "Small countries have few people." Germany, with her 82 million people, is not a small country in any European sense. On the world scale, however, Germany ranks only fourteenth after the Philippines (93 million) and Vietnam (86 million). Over 30 percent of Germany's citizens have a migration background. The German language, despite being the majority language with regard to native speakers in Europe, will not be able to achieve clear supremacy in Europe, let alone in any Asian belief structure, nor does the German culture it promotes. The German-Jewish connection before World War II was a winning formula for Nobel Prizes, but that, too, has slipped away forever.

Today, China and India want German cars, technology, and knowledge, but they certainly do not want German culture. When the Social Democratic Party of Germany under Chancellor Gerhard Schröder in the year 2000 over-confidently announced it would tap the vast market of two million Indian software programmers ("We want to hire 20,000 by the end of the year!"), only a tiny fraction of that, exactly 1,200 Indian experts, applied to Berlin. In the end, only 88 of them came. The idea that at any given moment, there are "millions" of colored people at the white man's beck and call is a textbook case of European hubris.

To sum up, it is highly unlikely, for the time being, that Germany, or ever smaller European states like France, Britain, or Italy could ever be a role model for India, Japan, Korea, or

China. In fact, it would be foolish to adopt the German way, or the French, or the British. To force Asia and say that any single European country should be a role model for its nations is a racist stance that we must never ever take again.

The Psychology of Communion

The bias of 'Western standard' – after all, the whole project of 'Cultural Anthropology,' eighteenth, nineteenth, and twentieth centuries' Orientalism, let alone the 'History of Sciences in China,' an objective presentation of "what China herself thought about her traditions" (Butler, 1927), are all *Western discipline*s – caused some difficulties for unabashed historians to distinguish between *genuine* Western thought and classy *adaptations* of East Asian or Hindu concepts in the West. There are some prominent examples of the latter: Jacques Derrida's 'différance,' Michel Foucault's 'archaeology,' Edmund Husserl's 'transcendental phenomenology,' even Jean-Paul Sartre's 'existentialism,' highly original as it is, all have

Orientalist themes (Moore, 2003). Some Western protagonists revealed their Asian sources; others did not (Wang, 2001).

Georg Hegel's 'philosophy of history,' 'Weltgeist' ('world-spirit'), and the 'great man theory,' all of which took Europe's intelligentsia by storm, were a blatant extension of Mahayana Buddhist concepts such as 'Brahmatmaikyam' (the merging of Brahman and Atman) and the Hindu tradition of 'Vardhamana Mahavira' (The Great Hero) or the 'Tirthankaras' (Sanskrit for 'fordmakers').

In *Die Welt als Wille und Vorstellung* (1819), Arthur Schopenhauer wrote (Abelson, 1993), "If I were to take the results of my philosophy as the standard of truth, I would have to consider Buddhism the finest of all religions."

Friedrich Nietzsche's concepts of 'Übermensch' (lit. 'over-man') and 'Meister- und Sklavenmoral' (lit. 'master- and slave-morality') are heavily influenced by Hindu concepts of 'vasudeva' ('super-human') and 'jatis' ('hereditary groups or castes'), while he elsewhere confessed, after having read Louis Jacolliot's 1876 translation of the *Manava Dharmasastra*, that the Vedic *Laws of Manu* was, in his opinion, the "epitome of all civic moral order" (Behler, 1987). Moreover, Martin Heidegger (1889-1976) and his philosophy of Western 'beingness and time' was a direct response to Eastern concepts of 'non-beingness and non-time' (May, 1996).

And then there was Adolf Hitler (1889-1945). Like Friedrich Nietzsche (1844-1900), Hitler worshipped might, and might was what he dreamt about when his utopian 'Third Reich' took shape in *Mein Kampf* (1925/26). Nazi ideology was deeply influenced by German Orientalism, which flourished from the eighteenth to twentieth centuries, and I am not just referring to the metaphysics of some Buddhist 'Swastika' as the chosen symbol of Aryan ascendancy and the spiritual conquest of India.

The idea of the 'Third Reich' did not, as many Western historians tend to believe, only derive from studying the Holy Roman Empire, or French or British colonial empires in their heydays. Far from it. Neither ancient nor recent, highly diversified European history had a precursor to the things outlined in the Nazi master plan: the Germans' obsession with Oriental themes and this so-called longing for the 'exotic other' romanticism, nostalgia for greatness, and rise to great power status during the years of the German Empire (Said, 1978; Zizek, 1997). All of this impelled the Germans to search for their identity and cultural legitimacy, e.g. Hellenic philosophical roots, the Holy Roman Empire of the German Nation, the Aryan invasion of India, the age of European Enlightenment, the invention of modern scholarship, the exploitation of Asian thought. They thus created a world history with Germany as its spiritual and cultural center.

The rational, analytical, deductive Germans, consciously or unconsciously indulging in a spiritual mission to make Europe 'coherent' and 'uniform,' actually wanted to *Easternize* it. By adopting the inductive Eastern ways, some historians believe German Orientalism had "helped to destroy Western self-satisfaction, and to provoke a momentous change in the culture of the West: the relinquishing of Christianity and classical antiquity as universal norms" (Marchand, 2001).

The Germans wanted to *undo* Europe's regional, provincial, fragmentary character, that is, to write an ethnocentric Aryan history. Similarly, in China they wrote the ethnocentric Chinese history that connects simultaneously to the past, present, and future, that worships its great ancestors and their deeds, that gives authority to memory and historians, that sees human action and its consequences as reigning over time, rather than just passing through time in discrete temporal units – days, hours, minutes. To the horror of their Western neighbors, the newly elected Nazis, well-educated in Classics, Philology, and Cultural Anthropology thanks to Humboldt's university reforms starting in the year 1810, *despised* the deductive, rational, and all-fabricated 'intellect,' and at the same time *idealized* their newly-found intuitive, spiritual, and all-human 'instinct.'

It comes as no surprise that even today, the average American Joe has great difficulty distinguishing between German-style totalitarianism and Soviet- or Maoist-style totalitarianism, and there is no blaming him for that. As Hannah Arendt convincingly put it: They were two sides of the same coin, not opposing philosophies (Arendt, 1973). Germany wanted to *undo* the East-West dichotomy and wanted the two great cultural modes to occupy the same space.

And it comes as no surprise either that to this day, the majority of Western scientists, who have never sufficiently studied the East-West dichotomy, ascribe history's darkest events to mere outer-world, materialistic circumstances like brainless *Youth Bulges* (Heinsohn, 2003; 2005), *Guns, Germs and Steel* (Diamond, 2003; 2006), or other material convulsions, while ignoring all the evidence that suggests that the ultimate cause of history's darkest events was an inner-world, monstrous, deadly *human psychology* – the communion of Eastern and Western souls:

European "discovery" of India brought the opportunity to appropriate its rich tradition for the sake of the Europeans' obsession to re-imagine their history and status. Many rival theories emerged, each claiming a new historiography. The new European preoccupation among scholars was to reinvent identities of various European peoples by suitably locating Sanskrit amidst other selective facts of history to create Grand Narratives of European supremacy [...] in order to fulfill their own ideological imperatives of reconciling theology with their self-imposed role of world ruler.

(Kapil Kapoor, 2001, here condemning the promoters of Aryan theories such as Max Müller [1823-1900])

What the German Orientalists and politicians prior to the Great Wars discovered – leaning towards Eastern-inflected concepts such as Mackinder's 'heartland theory' (1904), Max Müller's 'Aryan supremacy' (1892), and Nietzsche's prophetic 'Übermensch' (1885) – was that the Western hemisphere needed a domesticated ueber-race of Aryans in order to occupy Eurasia and counter the disciplined, ever-increasing, and expanding powers of the Eastern hemisphere. Germany feared the inductive, rising East, not her western or southern neighbors, among which she was already the dominant intellectual power. Germany was somehow right about the challenges from the East, as the Allies and the North Atlantic Treaty Organization indeed needed another 46 years (!) until the Cold War was won, a Pyrrhic victory, as it turned out: Today the West is helpless and in disbelief in the face of the until now peaceful rise of not one, recovering Russia, but of about a dozen new players: China, India, the nine 'Tiger States,' plus the world's second-largest economic superpower, Japan.

In order to understand 'history's darkest events' caused by an inner-world, monstrous, deadly psychology, the communion of Eastern and Western souls, we have to again address the topic of *Right* and *Tact*.

As it turned out, the Germans' pre-war master plan was hard, and physically impossible, to execute in the real world, but not at all difficult to grasp using our imaginations as serious students of world history today. What the Germans – in reference to what I said before about *Right* and *Tact* – did was *Right*, but *without Tact.* Now, before you protest against my claim that the Germans were "right," we should carefully examine the meaning of 'righteousness' in this respective European context. The Germans did the *right* thing, but not in a tactful manner. Order, discipline, submission in the name of unity was *Right*, so was the *unity of Europe* led by its most populous, industrious, and powerful people, the Germanic people. Was it not the Enlightenment thinker Jean-Jacques Rousseau (1712-1778) who suggested to Europeans that every individual must submit to the 'general will' and become an 'indivisible part' of the whole or the 'national will' (Rousseau, 1762)?

Striving for unification, as opposed to separatism, was the 'right' thing to do for Germany, the most populous nation of Europe. China was unified; so were the USA and India. But the Germans did not know how to do it; they did know all about *Right*, but did not know about *Tact*. They thought that scientific methods and powerful materialism could compensate for a lack of *Tact* and thus caused unbelievable suffering and pain. The Germans had to brutally bully all Europeans into submission, instead of *tactfully* leading them into submission. This is an example of the inner-world, monstrous, deadly psychology of communion: the Western analytical-deductive mindset of 'deconstruction' combined with Eastern intuitive-inductive theories of 'oneness.' This led to the Holocaust, just as the Japanese with their intuitive-inductive mindset, after adopting Western analytical-deductive theories, set out to destroy their neighbors with their newly won, uncontrollable power.

The Japanese were certainly different from the Germans; traditional Japanese culture was familiar with *Tact*. And, before the dawn of modernity, they knew about *Right*, too. Before the dawn of modernity, Japan knew that is was *not Right* for her to rule over the ancient and mighty Chinese, Russians, or Koreans – it wasn't *Right* for her to rule supreme over Asia. But when she adopted the Western analytical-deductive mindset, she ignored what was *Right* and set foot on the Asian continent. When Japan was confronted with the reality of things, that is was *not Right* for this tiny island to rule over mainland China, she panicked and threw away her *Tact*, slaying her prisoners of war (cf. the Rape of Nanking) just because this small island was neither physically nor psychologically able to rule (let alone to justify rule) over an ancient culture and hundreds of millions of Chinese, Koreans etc.

Similar to Germany's misery, this misery of Japan was initiated by the careless communion of the inductive Eastern and deductive Western souls, causing untold suffering and pain. Fortunately, when Russian and Chinese souls adapted to Western-minded Communism in the beginning, they refined it in the last minute, calling it Stalinism and Maoism. Yet look at what misfortune and destruction the communion of Eastern and Western souls still brought upon their own kin!

The German Holocaust, Japanese militarism, Soviet and Chinese Communism – all these carry gruesome warnings about what I meant by saying the ultimate cause of history's darkest events was an inner-world, monstrous, deadly psychology: the communion of inductive Eastern and deductive Western souls.

The main focus of academic attention in the analytical-deductive West about those darkest events in history seems to rest, how could it be much different, on the 'methods,' the 'what' and 'how' by which the suffering and pain were inflicted, not on the 'who.' *Who* actually committed these deeds? Regarding the 'methods,' the 'what' and 'how' of the German concentration camps and the heinous crimes of the Japanese, so much has already been written that I shall only add this observation: Despite the hypocrisy of Western moral educators regarding the unbelievably cruel methods used to annihilate the enemy, all those methods are the least difficult to comprehend for any serious student of history. We are making a fuss about nothing. On the contrary, a basic understanding of 'how' to use the cruelest methods available to destroy one's enemy, in this century, is the minimum requirement for any 14-year-old 'virtual commander' who plays a strategic computer game like *Warcraft* (Blizzard, 2001), where distinctive races fight for honor, resources, and territory. A basic understanding of this 'how' is also the only thing required to read about the battle between the races in a bestseller such as J. R. R. Tolkien's *The Lord of the Rings* (Shippey, 2002; Garth, 2005) or watch James Cameron's Hollywood blockbuster *Avatar* (2009), which basically retells the universal story of how much fun it is for the European civilization to destroy indigenous cultures for material gains, especially when those indigenous people look so different from us (in the movie, they have blue skin) and put up a good fight. Again, the *what* we did to them and the *how* we did it, be it in reality, be it in the books or movies, are quite irrelevant, because they are *entertainment* and we will always find ways to improve our ways and effectivity. What should really matter not only to psychologists and theologians, but to all scholars in the humanities is the *who*. Who commits the cruel deeds? And why? If we know about the source, we may find a cure.

Again, coldly analyzing the facts and methods of history's darkest events, the 'what' and 'how,' is *dehumanizing* and requires little intellectual effort. What could we possibly learn from it except doing it better next time? A *more* accurate understanding of what happened to the people of this world, to those who dominate and those who are being dominated, to all of us in our darkest times, can only be achieved by also looking at the '*who*,' i.e. by looking into our souls.

Having talked about the presence of *Right* and the absence of *Tact* of the Germans prior to the Great Wars, we must not forget to discuss another important component of the German mindset, namely the *Will* – the *Will* to make great things happen, the *Will to Power*.

As said elsewhere, Europe before history's darkest events was fractured, Balkanized, useless, *tactless*, and in moral decline. The only sense of unity came from the Church, but the self-interested, materialistic European nation states had left behind this source of spiritual unity in favor of independence, nationalism, and sovereignty. Then and before the Great Wars, who could ever possibly unite all Europeans in order to face the civilizations of the East? The British always knew what was

Right; it was not *Right* for them to set foot on the continent, nor to aspire to rule over Europe. In Europe, they made no great leaders either: The French were few in number, had a sorry history of defeat and failures against the British, and in any case, similar to the Scandinavian countries, could trace back their ancestors to tribes in the Germanic heartland.

The Germans of central Europe in the year 1930 were by far the most populous group in Europe, with over 60 million people within Germany, not counting Austria and the Germanic diasporas all over Europe. The Germans had been the discredited losers of World War I, stripped of all overseas colonies and one third of their former territory. With their enormous sense of righteousness, they naturally felt that their situation was not right, that no gang-up of (in their nationalistic view) mediocre European neighbor-states with their tinsel cultures should keep Europe small:

> *There is a Chinese saying that all mothers teach their children: Xiao Xin "make your heart small!" That really is the basic tendency of all later civilizations: I do not doubt the ancient Greeks would spot today's European self-inflicted reduction in size at first sight – this alone would be sufficient to disgust them.* (Friedrich Nietzsche, [1] 1909)

Nietzsche had his own vocabulary for the East-West dichotomy. He distinguished between two modes of culture: the (Western) individual – the rational, technical, cognitive, useful, and hierarchical *Apollonian*; and the (Eastern) collective – emotional, sexual, mystic, fertile, and revolutionary *Dionysian* (Nietzsche, 1872). Any reader knowledgeable in the history of thought will have noticed that pre-war Germany, in an incredible shift of paradigm later supervised by the Nazi party and its imitators and followers in Europe and beyond, had cultivated upon their soil for the first time ever an inherently *Apollonian*/Western culture with the acquired mindset of a collective, emotional, sexual, mystic, fertile, revolutionary *Dionysian*/Eastern soul. This had disastrous consequences for the well-being of Europe and the global community.

It is helpful to remind ourselves that there is a reason why so many of the above mentioned German thinkers were so admired among intellectual circles in the East, most notably in Japan (e.g. the Kyoto School, 京都派), India, but also in China: The intuitive Germans, from Goethe over Hegel, Schelling, Fichte, and Schopenhauer to Nietzsche and Heidegger were all pregnant with Oriental thought.

In sum, Eastern concepts have been borrowed and adapted throughout European history, sometimes for the worse (as in the case of pre-war Germany), but often for the better. However, the main standard throughout history remained Eurocentric. Asian values were communicated, often ridiculed, but never openly acknowledged. Whatever the East offered via its strange languages and spiritual terminology, it did not matter much unless it was translated and sealed for approval by the dominant civilization: the West. Why this Western 'verbal dominance' over the course of world history? We will discuss this in the next chapter.

Cultural Evolution

Let us imagine two people, *Mr. East* and *Mr. West*, who differ significantly in their attitudes, behaviors, and ways of perception. To find out why, let us use technical terms from 'Differential Psychology' to describe them. Mr. West is *more* rationally driven, while Mr. East is *more* intuitively driven. Although both could have developed the whole range of possible talents to a sufficient degree, yet each of them chose to display one set of particular talents more than the other. Given the limited time span of a single human life, many people may become excellent artists or brilliant scientists, but rarely does someone excel in both areas. Why? Because in our very competitive societies, our time and resources are limited; it is a very practical decision for Mr. East to do something different from Mr. West. Once that decision has been made, both will start cultivating their strengths, while neglecting their weaknesses. It is about finding one's niche, occupation, purpose, or destiny in life. The ideal time to make that practical decision is usually at an early age, and thus it not only depends on genetic factors or character traits, but is often heavily influenced by exterior factors such as family situation, parental support, and teachers. Thus, Mr. East became an excellent artist, while Mr. West became a brilliant scientist, because the former came from a family of artists, and the latter came from a family of scientists. If this applies to two individuals, Mr. East and Mr. West, why not for whole groups, even entire civilizations? After all, if the West were really so superior, how come that the East is still with us, and for so long? Surely, East and West *do* complement each other somehow.

Although Aristotle's *analytical-deductive method* (384 BC-322 BC) and Confucius' *intuitive-inductive method* (551 BC-479 BC) seem to be purely accidental, singular, isolated incidents, once they introduced those methods, one *more* scientific, the other *more* intuitive, the two methods helped shape their respective civilizations, and unintentionally pushed them apart into two different directions.

Anthropologists now teach us that powerful individuals or important texts that dictate or maintain certain group-level codes and behaviors can lead to the evolution of an efficient social system (Reynolds, 1983; Boyd & Richerson, 1992; Boyd, 2003; Mace, 2005). Contrary to popular belief, cultural evolution leads to social systems that are more stable than the Mendelian (genetic) ones, because culture is less sensitive to migration. That is believable, isn't it? All branches of Buddhism today – most of them found in Japan, China, and Korea – are based on Sakyamuni's teachings (c. 563 BC-483 BC) in Nepal, now forming the *Tipitaka Canon* (c. 100 BC) written down during the Fourth Buddhist Council in Sri Lanka/India. Buddhism slowly declined in India (c. 100-1192), revived in China (starting from c. 100 BC-AD 100), and has flourished ever since in Korea (from c. 372) and Japan (from c. 467). This example of 'cultural evolution' shows that any witness of change in turn may change his or her group's beliefs, learn new languages and ideas, or choose a new religion, thus promoting cultural evolution faster than that same group would be able to change its skin or eye color in genetic evolution (Mace, 2005).

Bearing in mind that groups influence or manipulate each other's development, cultural evolution does not necessarily work strictly alongside genetic evolution. Therefore, two societies may have developed a similar culture and value system but do not necessarily share the same density of certain racial phenotype, and vice versa (Reynolds, 1983; Cavalli-Sforza et al., 1994; Mace, 2005).

It is difficult to say who the greatest individual is in human history. But we do know what are the world's most best-selling books, although this will disappoint a lot of China-bashers: Number one is 毛主席语录 (*Mao Zhuxi Yulu, Quotations from Chairman Mao*), with over six and a half billion copies sold since its first publication in 1966. Number two is the Bible, with close to six billion copies sold since its first publication two millenia ago. Numbers three, four, and five again are Chinese books: 新华字典 (*Xinhua Zidian, Xinhua Dictionary*, 1957; 400 million), 毛主席诗抄 (*Mao Zhuxi Shichao, Chairman Mao's Poems*, 1966; 400 million), 毛主席文选 (*Mao Zhuxi Wenxuan, Selected Articles of Chairman Mao*, 1966; 252.5 million) (Wikipedia, 2008). No further comment necessary.

During the cultural evolution of the East-West dichotomy, whoever witnessed those important processes – in sociology we speak of formations – initiated by Aristotle and Confucius and their successors taught those new methods – in sociology we speak of variants – to another witness and so on. This way the new method or variant is replicated within that group. Generation after generation all imitate each other; we say they form logical or intuitive series. Confucius was continued by Mencius; Aristotle was continued by Plato; Jesus Christ was continued by Saint Paul etc.

Now, we might agree that Confucius was the initiator of what we now call Confucianism and the *Confucian Four Books and Five Classics* (四書五經, si shu wu jing) and that the pre-Confucian inductive method of the *I Ching* (易经) was the initiator of Confucius' *Great Learning* (大学, da xue). Furthermore, we could say that the following great Chinese philosophers somehow form a necessary series: Confucius [孔子] (551 BC-479 BC), Mo Zi [墨子] (470 BC-391 BC), Lao Zi [老子] (c. 400 BC), and Zhuang Zi [庄子] (370 BC-301 BC); or Zhang Zai [张载] (1020-1077), Cheng Yi [程颐] (1033-1107), Sima Guang [司马光] (1019-1086), Zhu Xi [朱熹] (1130-1200); Wang Fuzhi [王夫之] (1619-1692) and so on. Finally, we might agree that during the Warring States Period (战国时代, Zhanguo shidai, c. 500 BC-221 BC) the 'Hundred Schools of Thought'

(诸子百家, Zhuzi baijia) emerged in China – among others, Confucianism, Mohism, Daoism, Legalism, Logicism, Buddhism, and the Yin-Yang School. All those Chinese schools of thought, however isolated or original they claimed to be, nevertheless form a cultural succession, the so-called 'History of Chinese Thought' (just as the West has its own 'History of Western Philosophy'). And, as most Chinese thinkers usually cite their masters and prominent predecessors, we may ultimately be able to trace back the very origins of the Chinese tradition to the *I Ching*, also known as the Book of Changes, or, as far as the ancient sages are concerned, to the King Wu of Zhou (周武王, 1111 BC-1105 BC) and his brother, the Duke of Zhou (周公), also called the "God of Dreams" for his exceptional good governance. Therefore, in hindsight, the various Chinese schools of thought – even Chinese Buddhism that was first introduced via India and quickly Sinicized – share certain key Chinese characteristics (such as the concepts of 道 [*dao*] and 圣人 [*shengren*]), just as all Western philosophies share a common Greco-Roman and/or Judeo-Christian origin (such as the concept of 'philosophy' itself).

儒、释、道三教，譬如三个铺面挂了三个招牌，其实都是卖的杂货，柴米油盐都是有的，不过儒家的铺子大些，佛、道的铺子小些，皆是无所不包的.

Confucianism, Buddhism, Daoism… are like the signboards hung outside three shops, and although they sell mixed provisions, still there is nothing they don't stock in all the shops. (Liu E, 1909)

Once the foundations had been laid, what followed had to refer to its Confucian initiator(s). Even now, over 2,500 years after the *I Ching* [易经], *Lun Yu* [论语], or *Dao De Jing* [道德经], the Chinese people embrace the Confucian ideal of a 'harmonious society' (和谐社会, hexie shehui), 'oneness of man and heaven' (天人合一, tian ren he yi), and 'All under Heaven or Celestial Empire' (天下, tianxia). This relationship between Confucius, the 'inductive approach,' and the Chinese collective mind is so intimidating, that it makes me think that if there had been a great individual much earlier than the Duke of Zhou, Confucius, or the mystical Fu Xi, that same individual could have paved – similar to bottleneck situations in genetic evolution (Maddison et al., 2007) – the way for a continuous specialization of the Asiatic people in following the inductive path. This would be similar to how simple births/deaths of Buddhist sages may correlate quite neatly with the founding of different Buddhist subbranches (India) or their separation (China, Korea, and Japan). As a random example, in Japan, this led to the founding of the Jodo-shu School (浄土真宗, Pure Land) in 1133-1212 by Honen (法然, 1133-1212) and later Shinran (親鸞, 1173-1263).

The affinity with 'sages' and 'bodhisattvas,' that is, enlightened beings in the state of pre-Buddhahood, in all South-East and East Asian societies is well documented, but by no means uniform. Far from it, it is very regional, according to each country's historical context and ability to absorb new schools of thought. Maitreya (弥勒佛), the original 'next' Future Buddha, was over the centuries demoted to just another bodhisattva among the many bodhisattvas in the Hindu/Buddhist universe in India. In Tibet, more local, Tibetan deities were introduced, with Maitreya becoming ever less significant. In western China, where Buddhism contended with Daoism and Confucianism, traditional Chinese culture saw no need for a 'next' Buddha, and thus used the myth of the Chinese monk Budai (布袋) from ninth-century China during the Five Dynasties period as the personification of Maitreya. He is known in the West as the big-bellied, happy 'Laughing Buddha,' but he is actually not a real

Buddha. In Japan, Maitreya (Miroku) was in the end unable to retain his eminent position as prospective future Buddha, but instead became one of the 'Seven Gods of Fortune' (Shichi Fukujin, 七福神), often depicted riding on their ship, the Takarabune (宝船). If that allegorical ship would have set sail and crossed the Atlantic Ocean to the USA, what kind of promotion would the Enlightened One attain in the minds of the American people? Chances are he would become yet another wooden decoration in some giant IKEA warehouse. In fact, IKEA's Swedish headquarters already saw about 10,000 Hindus protesting against the great insult of "featuring a toilet seat Buddha" – that's right, a toilet seat adorned with a round-faced Buddha (AP Worldstream, 2002).

Next is the Confucian concept of 'shengren.' As the ideal human being, the shengren [圣人] is the highest member in the East Asian family-based value tradition, a sage that has the highest moral standards, or de [德], who applies the principles of ren [仁], li [礼], yi [义], zhi [智], and xin [信], and interacts with all people as if they were, metaphorically speaking, his family. The shengren in Confucianism are just as clearly defined and non-European as the Buddhas in Buddhism are; yet, as of today, the Western public is ignorant about the shengren. Worse, people have no way of knowing that they don't know shengren. That's because when the European missionaries came to China to preach the Gospel in the seventeenth century, they translated key Chinese concepts into biblical and philosophical (European) terminology. Accordingly, people in Europe were taught in school that there were 'philosophers' and 'saints' all over Asia; yet, upon reflection, evidently there wasn't a single Buddha, bodhisattva, or shengren in Europe. Think. What is that probability? Whose version of 'History' (with a capital H) are we taught? As Howard Zinn once said, "If something is omitted from history, you have no way of knowing it is omitted" (Zinn, 1980)

The evolution of different cultures is real (Dunbar, 1999; Diamond, 2003), so is the evolution of written texts (Howe et. al., 2005), language (Gray et. al., 2000; Mace, 2005; Haspelmath, 2005), and religion (Reynolds, 1983). The only major obstacle in anthropology – as opposed to archaeology – is to locate manuscripts or records written before the fifth or fourth millennium BC (Fischer, 2005).

After so much 'what,' it is high time to ask 'why?' Why has the evolution of cultures resulted in this equilibrium of the two great cultural systems, the Occidental and the Oriental one, the inductive East and the deductive West, with no third great cultural system? Possibly because a third cultural system *does not exist*.

All available evidence speaks for itself, yet let us listen to another Nobel laureate:

中华传统文化的一大特色是归纳法，可是没有推演法。其中归纳法的来源是什么？"易者象也"，"圣人立象以尽意"，"取象比类：，"观物取象"都是贵穿《易经》的精神内。都是归纳法，是向上求整体"象"的方法。徐光启在翻译了欧几里德的几何原本以后，了解到推演法一个特点就是"欲前后更置之不可得"。就是一条一条推论不能次序颠倒。这跟中国传统不一样。中国传统对于逻辑不注意，说理次序不注意，要读者自己体会出来最后的结论。

The inductive method is a major feature of traditional Chinese culture, but not so the deductive method. What is the source of the inductive method in China? All these concepts of 'Yimutology' are described in the Book of Changes. *These are inductive methods to infer from the particular to the universal 'form.' When Xu Guangqi translated Euclid's* Elements of Geometry, *he immediately understood the strength of the deductive method: "The conclusion has to follow from the premises and not otherwise." That direction of the reasoning process in the deductive method cannot be reversed. Chinese tradition, however, was different. Chinese scholars did not pay much attention to logical order; the reader would make sense of everything once he understood the final conclusion.* (Yang Zhenning [杨振宁], 2004)

Recently, three dozen prestigious professors from Peking University have completed *A History of the Chinese Civilization* (中华文明史, 2006) after six years of hard work (Yuan Xingpei, 2006). After reading some parts of the book, I did not find a political or historical framework that could ever be considered in line with the political or historical framework of European thought. That has always been the case in Chinese history, whether in the *Records of the Warring States*, compiled in the Han Dynasty, or in the *Records of the Grand Historian Si Maqian* (司马迁, c. 145 BC-90 BC). In China, there has always been an entirely different approach to history, its people, and the notion of time (Wu, 2007; 2008):

> *So, we should just gently shift the frame from theoretical "time" to concrete "history," and China's rich millenarian blood will at once throb into our veins, to flood our pages. We will engage in lively inter-communications with all the historic Wise, popular and academic among our celebrated Five Chinese Races. We learn from ancient Sages, to revise and add to them.* (Wu Kuang-Ming, 2007)

In the history books of ancient China, which often still influence the style and way of thought of today's textbooks, there are generalizations over generalizations. In these books you will also find the notion that China is a single entity, more generalizations, the idea that all Chinese think and feel the same, that all China is 'one,' all people are 'one,' all have 'one' moral code, and that 'China' pits herself and all her history against the 'other' barbarians surrounding China (Nolde, 1966; Huan et al., 1997). To the typical Western-educated scholar, studying history in China is often a painstaking process – many experts despair at the lack of regionalism, objectivity, glossaries, reference material, logical structure, punctuation, and useful introductions. Instead, sinologists will encounter beautiful adjectives, splendid analogies, lovely sceneries, ethical evaluations, moving dialogues, personal comments, and practical moral lessons. In fact, in Chinese literary tradition (and this is important), if a man's intellect is able to recognize the 'interconnectedness' and the 'greater whole,' this would make him a great scholar, a true gentleman, while all other lesser men will almost inevitably lose themselves in unnecessary details:

公都子問曰："鈞是人也，或為大人，或為小人，何也？"孟子曰："從其大體為大人，從其小體為小人。"曰："鈞是人也，或從其大體，或從其小體，何也？"曰："耳目之官不思，而蔽於物，物交物，則引之而已矣。心之官則思，思則得之，不思則不得也。此天之所與我者，先立乎其大者，則其小者弗能奪也。此為大人而已矣。"

Kung Tu Tzu said, "If all men are equal, how is it that there are greater and lesser men?" Mencius said, "Some follow their greater part, and some follow their lesser part." "Why do some follow their greater part and some follow their lesser part?" Mencius said, "The organs such as the eye and ear cannot discriminate and are thus confused by things. Things are interconnected with other things, which lead one further away. The function of the mind is to discriminate – if you discriminate, you will attain it. If you don't discriminate, you won't attain it. These are what Heaven has bestowed upon us. If you first establish yourself in the greater part, then the small part cannot be snatched away from you. This is the essential of being a great man." (Mencius, 6A.15)

Before the end of the nineteenth century, in China there was no philosophy as such, no historiography or literature, only the Classics [径], Masters [子], and Historical Records[诗] (Sisci, 2008). The authority of the living was derivative, depending upon the authority of the masters, who no longer were among the living (Arendt, 1993). Only by memorizing the classics could a great man be able to comprehend the depth and complexity of human existence (Li Wai-Yee, 2008). This is true of China today, where commentators on ancient Chinese texts still often treat them as a closed system, with complete inner coherence, and assume 'pan-signification.' This is reflected, of course, in politics – as if the only task of the past was to safeguard the future grand unity and authority of China today, despite distorting history (Ge, 2001).

As experience has shown, no man or woman of importance in the Western world (sinologists excepted) is going to read a Chinese history book unless it is translated into English, that is, unless it is incorporated into 'Western history,' which is nothing less than 'world history' itself. Since not a single non-Western society, it seems, can produce an alternative to the world history that the West would be able to read, it could be tempting to pronounce all other histories 'dead.' Since the striving for different histories, or different versions of it, truly has come to an end, leaving only one 'world history,' Westerners might as well continue this as 'The Chronicles' or simply 'twenty-first century, twenty-second century,… etc.,' (counting from zero, which marks the anniversary of the birth of Jesus Christ and the beginnings of Christianity), thus ending the histories of all other (Confucian, Hindu, Islamic, Buddhist etc.) cultures as we used to know them (Fukuyama, 1992).

With just one history left, the Western hemisphere is going to dictate how it is written. The content, however, might be saying otherwise, as we shall see in the next chapter.

A Copernican Revolution

Looking at 'world history' – on the one side, the rational, incredible West that ends all other 'histories' and promotes the universal language, English, and on the other side the intuitive, incredible East that closes the historic circuit and integrates the universal language, English – in this twenty-first century, it is nevertheless the East that holds a considerable advantage. It is the *bigger phenomenon*.

Let us make no mistake: Communism and Capitalism were made for *scale* and the *masses*, and scale and masses are now in *Asia*. So are *numbers*. So are the world's greatest challenges such as economic stability, food shortages, pollution, environmental destruction, population explosions, youth bulges, and terrorism, all of which are demanding more global attention.

The *bigger*, or, as we are talking about history, shall we say the *greater* the phenomenon a theory describes, the greater that theory becomes. In the past, great phenomena often happened in isolation and did not automatically call for global attention. For example, the intellectual output of India is legendary; her civilization is older than the Greeks' (c. 3300 BC). India taught the West how to count; she conquered and dominated China, Korea, and Japan *culturally* (I am talking, of course, about the influence of Buddhism) "for twenty centuries without ever having to send a single soldier across her border" (Hu Shi [胡适], 1891-1962). She was the source of enlightenment for Europe, and the main source of German philosophy in the last three centuries. Similarly, China during the early Ming Dynasty (1368-1421) accounted for roughly 25 to 30 percent of the world's gross domestic product, while the combined productivity of the European nations did not exceed 20 percent (Needham, 1963; Maddison, 2006; Spence, 2001). Once the potential of those 'great phenomena,' those two great Eastern giants, had been realized in the West, that indeed could have been among the most important reasons why the small European states – with all their trials of Eastern expansion, colonialism, and imperialism – always seemed to have a greater interest in Asia. Those European states were interested in Asia's technologies, wealth, land, and resources, more than the other way around, but this, of course, is just speculation.

What is not speculation is that Europe never paid enough attention to where it gets more complicated: the religious, ethical, and sociological wisdom of the East. Or better, that religious, ethical, and sociological wisdom that had been created by the East, not indirectly by the West. Today, times have changed, the great wheel of fortune has turned, and China, India, and the other Asian states provide golden opportunities for theoretical innovations and the creation of new values, more than in any other part of the world (Lin, 2006). Thus, the twenty-first century is very likely to be the century of the Chinese economist and the Indian computer scientist, as both countries already produce more university graduates than the USA or the European Union. The USA and Europe already heavily rely on tens of thousands of Asian graduates and those priceless connections these graduates offer for the future competitiveness of Western societies.

Having established that Asia, in this century, evidently constitutes a greater phenomenon than Europe or the USA, why then should anyone think that Chinese culture, or any other East Asian culture for that matter, is a pitiful victim of Westernization?

On the contrary, isn't it the case that not the West but the East is now nurturing the content of 'world history'? Where are today's Western politicians, historians, and men of letters who stand up to the truth? 'World history' is becoming genuine, not European, let alone American, which is but an extension of the Eurasian people's achievements. Are Western leaders afraid that their countrymen are not mature enough to face the 'other humanity,' the East, unless they are assured it is an inferior one?

China had numerous invaders, like the Liao (907-1125), the Jurchen (during Northern Song, 1115-1234), Yuan/Mongols (1271-1368), and the Manchus (1644-1911), yet she absorbed them all. India in the tenth century alone was invaded 17 times by the Muslim Mahmud Ghaznavi and his successors, by the Mongol Empire (1221-1327), and, starting from the fifteenth century onwards, by the Portuguese, Dutch, French, and British imperialists. Both China and India have either assimilated or expelled each and every invader. Furthermore, there are Russia, Vietnam, Thailand, Korea, Myanmar, and Indonesia – none of these places appears as if the West had 'taken over.' Even Japan, the *American Geisha Ally* (Shibusawa, 2006), is so entirely different in her spiritual, cultural, ideological, and psychological makeup, that to call her a Western progeny would be an insult to Japan, her long history, and her fine people. Lastly, no Muslim or Arab state, not even the occupied Iraq or Afghanistan, strike me as Western 'colonies' either. Quite the opposite: Many people secretly think it was Islam which destroyed U.S. hegemony by attacking the Twin Towers and provoking the disproportional response of the USA, and that it is Islam and the Middle East which are now the forces to be reckoned with. Moreover, many Westerners think that Islamic culture is now 'besieging Europe' by presenting itself as an alternative cultural mode (Minority-Info, 2008).

What is this so-called process of 'Westernization,' if not the destruction or heavy manipulation of non-Western cultures? It is an exclusive treatment and reserved for the East. No one would think the West is westernizing itself. The East is studying the ways of the deductive West. It learns, internalizes, and gets stronger; I ask: What did the West learn from the inductive East to get wiser?

Not much, because it is not in the nature of the West to easily slip into the role of a student if it had been the master previously. That particular, aggressively progressive element of the materialistic-driven 'West in the East' has always been, educationally speaking, hopelessly misguided and short-sighted: In the end, a few European colonial administrators had either to comply with local culture (because Chinese, Japanese, Hindu etc. civilizations are often quite overwhelming to the tiny European cultures, and hard to change), use violence, or else, if they didn't use force, the Western occupiers had to leave for good – 'good' as in 'de-colonialism.' Without the use of manipulative forces against it, the East is morally superior. It is the true master of humankind. It emanates humanity itself. And the West hates it for that.

But the West never lost its self-confidence when it came to thinking that it was superior. Naturally, the pattern never changed, and the destructive, dividing-and-conquering Europeans kept coming back, and they are still coming back today (in their latest guise as the war-loving, self-righteous Americans). Now, they are not necessarily wielding swords and guns, but pens and patents; all the same, the West is now all about the East: World history is now all about great phenomena; world history is about the final universal 'oneness,' and the key to it is kept in the East.

Understandably, there is a most delicate degree of difference between let us say the prophet tempting the disciple and the disciple tempting the prophet; or: Human subjectivity deluding the world's objectivity and the world's objectivity deluding human subjectivity. Does not the East-West relationship, after its great derailment, face a similar dilemma too? Is it not high time for a shift of paradigm, a 'Copernican Revolution' in sociology, similar to that of Galileo in astronomy and that of Kant in metaphysics? During the 2,500 years of the East-West discourse we were tempted to believe that the human universe consists of the West at its core with all the other cultures revolving around this core. 'World history' worked fine that way.

Now, after having compiled so much evidence here, I am no longer convinced about that Western core. From the Eastern point of view, distant, peripheral Europe and the USA had the historical sense of mission to manipulate the East – the core. In physics, the core is always the most passive, most unwavering element. *Passive* and *unwavering* are precisely how the West perceives the East.

According to the definition above, Europe and the USA are active, peripheral forces revolving around whatever passive and immovable matter makes up the core of the human universe – like two hands molding a precious vase. However, the deductive West did not add any substance. It only formed, divided, conquered, ruled for a time; it invented thousands of new rules and regulations, stuck its fingers into the clay, and then did not know what to do next. It had no sense for Eastern form, substance, or spirituality. Alas, so bad was the West at building human relationships, be it by dispatching missionaries, conquerors, soldiers, bankers, or businessmen, that it merely left its fingerprints in the clay, emotional scars, but nothing that could ever transform the East into West.

There is a very active Western part: Some Western nations fought tooth and nail on Eastern soil during the Cold War, and now the West is back again with thousands of business contracts and globalizing catechisms. Asia is indeed very busy, busy studying all those new theories and techniques from the various Western 'invaders,' a lot more so than the invaders could possibly learn or could possibly be willing to learn from the East. Yet, all the same, it is the inductive East that attracts all these energies, all this Western attention. This pattern of Western nations revolving around Asia makes me think that it is the East that is at the core, in other words: The East, roughly since the second half of the twentieth century, has not only become the world's greatest phenomenon, but has also, slowly, shifted to the center of gravity of world affairs.

This shift of gravity is recognized by ever more European historians and scholars who now feel incomplete, not to say incompetent, if they haven't seen or experienced China. Some already predict the *Union of Chinese and Western Ethics* (Deng, 1999), with the Western idea of 'human rights' and the Chinese idea of 'human responsibility forming a new universal ethic: "Equilibrium between freedom, equality and participation does not simply happen, but must be re-established again, and again" (Küng, 1998).

The East and the inductive ways in which it excels are seen as the solution to humankind's problems: 'oneness.' And the West feels incomplete without it. If this world is truly to become a more stable, peaceful, albeit more complicated, 'integrated' place, a better place, as everyone now seems to believe it should, then the 'integration-based' East and the inductive way are not only destined to play a greater role in all human and world affairs, but must also form the core.

The Problem with Nature

一天地万物为一体。

Forming one body with heaven, earth and myriad things.
(Wang Yangming, 1472-1529)

Since the more inductive East and the more deductive West are both part of a gigantic ecosystem called Earth, it is important to understand how the two cultural hemispheres traditionally regarded their relationship with what truly matters to all of us: nature.

Given that the *analytically-based, deductive West* has the advantage of "processing information in a linear manner, that is from top to bottom, it collects a myriad of pieces, lines them up, and arranges them in a logical order before drawing the conclusions," it is clearly the dominant hemisphere when it comes to articulate, explain, and write down human history (brain.web, 2007).

The *integration-based, inductive East*, on the other hand, "processes from bottom to top, holistically. It starts with the answer. It sees the big picture first, the great harmony, not the details" (brain.web, 2007).

As a consequence, the deductive Western hemisphere is "not only thinking in a linear manner, processes in sequences, but is also a list maker, enjoys making master plans, and learns in sequences" (brain.web, 2007). Western culture is "a good speller who makes rules to follow, works in the linear and sequential processing of math and scientific methods" (brain.web, 2007).

By contrast, the inductive Eastern hemisphere processes information randomly. "It flips from one tack to another, it will get just as much done, but perhaps without having addressed priorities. It pays attention to coherence, greater meanings, illustrations and feelings" (brain.web, 2007). Its memory is connected to "emotions and feelings, not dealing with things the way they are with reality but with ideal concepts" (brain.web, 2007).

The inductive East, which naturally has got a glimpse of the 'whole picture,' is well aware of the job the deductive Western hemisphere is doing in Asia by deconstructing and manipulating the world and all things:

- *The West is linear, sequential, concrete, logical, verbal, and reality-based*

However, the deductive West, which experiences the world as being made up of a myriad of little details, is not aware of the Eastern hemisphere's goal of striving for a coherent 'wholeness' and 'interconnectedness':

- *The East is holistic, random, symbolic, intuitive, non-verbal, and fantasy-oriented*

A similar East-West comparison has been made by Li Dazhao [李大钊] (1888-1927), philosopher and co-founder of the Communist Party of China:

东洋文明主静，西洋文明主动，

一个动，一个静，这是一点。

东方是为自然的，西方是人为的；

东方是安息的，西方是战争的；

东方是消极的，西方是积极的；

东方是依赖的，西方是独立的；

东方是苛按的，西方是突进的；

东方是因袭的，西方是创造的；

东方是保守的，西方是进步的；

东方是直觉的，西方是理智的；

东方是空想的，西方是体验的；

东方是艺术的，西方是科学的；

东方是精神的，西方是物质的；

东方是灵的，西方是肉的；

东方是向天的，西方是立地的；

东方是自然支配人闻的，西方是人闻征服自然的。

Eastern civilization is static,

while Western civilization takes initiative;

One is active, while the other is passive, so much for that.

The East harmonizes with nature; the West conquers it;

The East is tranquil; the West is aggressive;

The East is introverted; the West is extroverted;

The East is dependent; the West is independent;
The East is reserved; the West is advancing;
The East is submissive; the West is creative;
The East is conservative; the West is progressive;
The East is intuition; the West is reason;
The East is spiritual; the West is empirical;
The East is humanistic; the West is scientific;
The East is mind; the West is matter;
The East is spirit; the West is substance;
The East is inductive; the West is deductive;
The East takes man and nature as inseparable parts;
the West takes man as the conqueror of nature.
(Li Dazhao, 2006)

Li Dazhao's observations are in line with how Western scientists generally perceive themselves and their abusive relationship with nature:

Only let mankind regain their rights over nature, assigned to them by the gift of God, and obtain that power, whose exercise will be governed by right reason and true religion.
(Francis Bacon, 1620)

The separation of knowledge from ethics, or let us say 'value-free knowledge,' is what most obviously distinguished the Greek/Hellenistic/European civilization from all the others. For the deductive West, everything in the universe can be considered a potentially useful object that must be studied and manipulated so as to serve 'man and his cause.' This 'man and his cause,' in the good old days of the British Empire, meant, of course, the 'British aristocracy and its cause.' But during the European Renaissance, this had quickly turned into 'Western man and his Western cause.'

'Western man and his Western cause' – this was about as far as it could be stretched. Enough human beings and territory were left out so that the scientific, deduction-based West could fulfil its mission, namely, to force the entire material world and everything non-Western to submit.

The Western 'scientific way' implies that there must be a non-scientific way, or just a 'non-scientific other' – nature and the 'other people' who value unity with nature. Nature and the traditional-minded people who side with nature are thus, by definition, at the wrong side of the 'man-conquers-nature' equation and must therefore be totally subjugated, deconstructed, divided, and manipulated by their scientific conqueror.

The playing out of opposing ideas and attitudes in world history thus strikingly resembles the battle between the differences of the right and left hemisphere of the human brain, whose power relationship is never quite symmetrical and indeed, between the ages, may swing like a pendulum. As Iain McGilchrist argued in his book *The Master and his Emissary: The Divided Brain and the Making of the Western World* (2011), both cerebral hemispheres entertain "whole, self-consistent versions of the world." The left hemisphere, the rigid, analytical, deductive one (technically slightly inferior because of its lack of any inclusive, holistic view, thus rightly called the "Emissary") suppressed the right hemisphere – its true "Master" – and "carried us further into the territory of the left hemisphere's world." That is how, according to the neurosciences, the manipulative Western hemisphere came to dominate world history.

In sum, to any non-Western observer, the West and its deeply rigid, intolerant 'scientific way' appears to be inherently violent (Nandy, 1989).

Asia, and by that I mean virtually all societies from the Russians over the Indians to the Muslims, Chinese, and Japanese, by definition had all been on the receiving end of 'world history.' They could help row, but not steer that boat. In an allegorical, Faustian sense, the political philosophers and scientists Francis Bacon (1561-1626), Thomas Hobbes (1588-1679), and Adam Smith (1723-1790) were among those great Western Enlightenment philosophers trading the Western conscience for the power it meant over those who still had to make a compromise with their conscience.

Until the final Faustian 'reckoning,' the Western powers, through all those centuries, could almost frivolously humiliate every other society on Earth until all ethical grounds were lost. Meanwhile, the very Eastern humanitarian notions of 'wholeness,' 'harmoniousness,' and 'oneness' became meaningless and undesirable to the average Western mind. What is most disturbing, however, is this: Even the slightest sign of 'wholeness,' 'harmoniousness,' and 'oneness' is now reminding the West of its past 'failures' and 'shame,' and thus, in the eyes of any analytical-deductive Westerner, must be avoided at all costs.

The final reckoning was considered imminent. In Mahatma Gandhi's words, it was only a matter of time until that 'other,' be it nature or man, subtly strikes back at the tormentor and destroys the illusion that only Western sciences are valid: "This [Western] civilization is such that one only has to be patient, and it will be self-destroyed" (Gandhi, 1938).

Gandhi was exaggerating; he did not believe that the West would simply destroy itself, or be destroyed by others, or that sciences would become invalid. But he believed in Eastern concepts of positive 'value-creation' and 'non-violence' that – in the long run – like all Eastern concepts of 'tolerance,' 'wholeness,' or 'oneness' – would appeal to the Western imperialists' sense of shame. And so they did:

> 人不可以無恥。無恥之恥，無恥矣。
> *A person cannot do without shame. If you are ashamed of your shamelessness, you will not need to be ashamed.*
> (Mencius, 7A.6)

It is the old pattern again: If the West searches for the *power over nature (matter)*, it is the East that searches for the *power over man (mind)*, and it is the healthy equilibrium that would benefit both of them and thus all of us.

Sadly, the analytical West is still patronizing 'its' spiritual East. The facts have changed. Global power has shifted, but the Western feelings of total superiority still linger. That is why the otherwise easily predictable rise and dominance of integration-based Asia in the twenty-first century still appear unlikely to most Europeans, even today.

Truths and Values

The products of human reasoning are always artificial. Initially, any original state does not make much sense to us nor does it seem useful until it has been transformed into an artificial state. There are only two modes of reasoning: Deductive reasoning will create an artificial product of certain but valueless truth. Inductive reasoning will create an artificial product of value but uncertain truth. The function of human reasoning is to produce two artificial things: truths and values.

Ideology

Based on its analytical, deduction-based approach and narrow views on the complexities of nature and history, the West lost sight of holistic, long-term future relationships, consciously or unconsciously indulging in the uncertainties and banalities of a postmodern, utterly deconstructed, and individualistic world. The East itself has not yet encountered this post-modern insecurity, and, as I will argue, it does not necessarily have to.

After Modernism (c. 1880-1950), which is understood as the age of totalities, essentialisms, and meta-narratives, Western societies had deconstructed all those past meta-narratives and entered the age of Post-modernism (c. 1950-2000) (Hutcheon, 1989). For some Eastern observers it seemed that in certain areas of analytical inquiry, the West was approaching its limits. Could there be anything smaller than Werner Heisenberg's smallest possible particles, the 'quarks'? What is the meaning of anything once everything is deconstructed?

西方的自然科学走的是一条分析的道路，越分越细…而对这些细节之间的联系则缺乏宏观的概括。
Western science has walked down the analytical path; the more it deduced, the smaller became the deducible…and (they) lost the macroscopic general perspective about how those details were related to each other.
(Ji Xianlin, 2006 [5])

Man faces a serious problem in the modern world because science has pursued the objective method of cognition and has analyzed and classified phenomena until we are left with only the pieces. (Tsunesaburo Makiguchi, in Brannen, 1964)

Werner Heisenberg's 'Uncertainty Principle' (1926), Kurt Goedel's 'Incompleteness Theorems' (1931), Ludwig Wittgenstein's 'Language Games' (1926), Edmund Husserl's 'Distress in Meaning' (1970), which he crowned with *The Crisis of European Sciences*, Jacques Derrida's 'Deconstructionism' (1960), Claude Lévi-Strauss' 'Bricolage' (1962), Edward Norton Lorenz's 'Chaos Theory' (1792), and the 'butterfly-effect,' the whole idea of Franz Boa's 'Cultural Relativism' (1942), meaning that all beliefs are valid and truth relative itself – all of those *end-of-meaningful-science theories* contributed to undermine our belief in a society's certainty, consistency, and continuity. If you are preoccupied with minutiae, after a century it gets to you: Secular Western societies therefore left it all to the individuals and their individual experiences to decide how to make sense of the world, and what to do with their minuscule lives.

The spiritual East, however, is different:

Ganga ca yamuna caiva godavari sarasvati; narmada sindhu kaveri stranar-atham prati-grhyatam.
I am taking a bath with all these rivers Ganga, Yamuna, Godavari, Narmada, Indus, Kaveri.

同一个世界,同一个梦想
One world, one dream.

The "Bath Sutra" of the Urdhvamnaya Tantra, which exists in various forms all across the Indian subcontinent, is a harmless spiritual song about the perceived unity of India and her now 1.2

billion people. The Chinese slogan for the 2008 Beijing Olympic Games is derived from 同一个中国 (one unified China), and thus not only confirms the ancient Confucian concept of 'tianxia' (天下, All under Heaven) or Dong Zhongshu's 'he er wei yi' (合而为一, unite and become one), but also subscribes to China's two famous policies: a) that the world should embrace (Confucian) harmony, which alleges that China's dream is everyone else's dream, too; and b) that China is indeed 'one' nation, including all her minorities and vital, problematic regions like Taiwan, Tibet, and Xinjiang. To my knowledge, there is no equivalent of such a spiritual – seemingly naïve – sense of unity in recent European history.

In contrast, Western societies, after a long history of assertiveness and expansion, so it seems, do not conquer anymore; they converge. While in the analytically-based West today it is inevitably the minuscule individual in multiculturalism (European Union, USA, Australia, Canada, New Zealand), in the integration-based East it is still the collective nation in numbers (China, India, but also Russia, Japan, Vietnam, Thailand, Korea, and the Middle East).

It is the old problem of either seeing the trees or seeing the forest, as reflected in the following two statements:

From each according to his ability, to each according to his needs. (Karl Marx, 1875)

and

有的国家占的篇幅多一点，有的少一点。这只事实求足。
Some countries take up more space, others less. That is simply how things are. (Ji Xianlin, 2006 [6])

The former quote suggests a philosophy for the individual (each tree) and hence implies the notion of *self-interest* and *limitation*; the latter suggests a philosophy for the masses (the whole forest) and hence implies *public-spiritedness* and *certainty*.

Long-term vision and constancy, as we have seen, are intrinsic values of integration-based Eastern societies:

其实世上本没有路，走的人多了，也便成了路。
As more people are walking all the time, in the same spot, a path appears. (Lu Xun, 1981)

In 50 years from now Iran, through political consistency, is projected to have one hundred million citizens (and possibly the atom bomb). Turkey, by then, is going to be Europe's biggest negotiating partner with the East, and, if accepted into the European Union, it will be its most populous nation with about 95 million people, in addition to the diaspora of almost 10 million Turks living scattered throughout the European Union. Vietnam, with its projected 120 million citizens, could become as populous as France and Great Britain combined. On a political level, the Communist Party of China has already more members than Germany's population, and since 2006, the Shanghai Cooperation Council has been the largest regional grouping in the world (and, it should be noted, without U.S. presence), not the North Atlantic Treaty Organization. Jairam Ramesh, former secretary of India's Congress Party's Economic Affairs Department, voiced this simple truth:

We [Indians] must examine our brains, if we are not capable to lead one billion people to become the world's third largest economy! (Jairam Ramesh, 2002)

Although some Europeans have analyzed the problem of declining native populations and accepted their ethnic decline, India, Pakistan, Turkey, Iran, Indonesia, Vietnam, the Arab

League with its 22 member states, Vietnam, Bangladesh, as well as other nations have no inclination towards state birth control, and China, facing a demographic aging problem, is reconsidering its one-child policy. Having too many workers is not China's problem, because it could always export more diasporas to Siberia, Africa, the Middle East, or Australia to expand the Chinese world.

The birth rates in European countries in the first decade of the new millennium were merely 1.3 in Germany, 1.29 in Italy, and 1.5 in France. According to the United Nations Population Division, on top of the world's population of 6.5 billion, we are expecting an additional 2.85 billion human beings in the next 50 years (UN Population Division, 2007), apparently none of them statistically white (although not necessarily non-Western). The percentage of white European descendants worldwide will shrink (relatively) from 8 percent at the turn of the millennium to just 2 percent 50 years later, down from 30 percent a century ago. With the exception of some Anglophone nations, notably the USA, Canada, New Zealand, and Great Britain, which will all increase in number due to massive immigration, the remaining European societies are showing a remarkable disinterest in their own *voluntary* decline, not to say ethnic and cultural suicide.

If there is going to be a 'world democracy' today, with each world citizen having exactly one vote, the declining Europeans had better unite with the neighboring Muslim world or else simply become irrelevant – if not to say impotent – in international politics. Anger, awe, fear, and the strange feeling of intimidation are relatively new to European intellectuals, but now suggested by the facts.

The last time European culture had been "seriously slackened to its bones" was when the Romans assimilated the Greeks around 300 years before the birth of Jesus Christ (Sisci, 2008). The rise of the East is now real and inevitable.

Having established that after the second half of the twentieth century the influence of the East is being felt everywhere, the question remains: "Who exactly is *the West*?"

Some say it is the Northern hemisphere, others say it is the white man; still others claim it is the First World, the developed world, or just the 'elite.' Surely we can find a better definition. I have one: The West, as I see it, has been victorious. That's why Japan wisely joined the club after 1900 when she defeated Russia and invaded China, Korea, Taiwan, and Indonesia. In spite of being defeated in World War II, she became the world's second biggest market economy after the USA. In 2004, China finally challenged the West too by overtaking Great Britain in terms of gross domestic product and became the fourth biggest market economy. In 2009, China overtook Germany, and two years later she surpassed Japan and is now the second largest economy on Earth. With India surpassing Great Britain's gross domestic product last year, has the West become nothing more than a mere geographical entity?

But geography is also misleading if one looks at any Asian map of the world: The USA lies to the East. It is only natural to conclude that the only distinction between East and West that matters today, as I said before, is their different modes of thinking. Also, due to the declining population in the West, a number of Easterners will (voluntarily or not) immigrate – not to conquer the declining West, but to strengthen the equilibrium. And equilibrium it will be, for to reform either side's civilization would mean, let us make no mistake, to discount that side's history, beliefs, and ancestors…everything.

Gender

Almost alone among barbarians they (the Germanic people) are content with one wife, except a very few among them, and these not from sensuality, but because their noble birth procures for them many offers of alliance.
(Tacitus, AD 92)

In the preceding chapters I talked about the common metaphor of culture as a living being (e.g. Oswald Spengler, 1922; Arnold Toynbee, 1958 etc.). In this chapter I go further by exploring the gender, sexual orientation, and maturity of that culture.

Among the many things that impressed Marco Polo in the thirteenth century, and what captured his readers' imagination throughout the centuries, is the absolute correct observation that a Mongol man, like the Mussulman, could take as many wives as he wanted: "When a husband leaves his wife to go on a journey for more than twenty days, as soon as he has left, she takes another husband, in this she is fully entitled to do by local custom. And the men, wherever they go, take wives in the same way" (Polo, 2007).

Now, I believe Marco Polo often confused the Mussulmen with the Mongols, and the Mongols with the common Chinamen (of whom there were countless clans), as there were many hundreds of cultures existing side by side in thirteenth century Cathay (China). The Mongols took over Cathay and established the Yuan dynasty (1264-1368) under Kublai Khan, who ruled from his court in Beijing, but they did not introduce polygamy in China. Far from it: Although polygamy was accepted in many societies around the globe, nowhere was it as common as in Asiatic societies. However, by far more popular was the phenomenon of concubinage, that is, the maintenance of mistresses.

Concubinage does not mean having multiple wives, like in traditional polygamy, and it is certainly not a form of prostitution either. I will discuss this shortly. Having multiple wives, as long as a man could afford such a costly status symbol, was common in Hindu societies, too (the mythical Krishna had 16,108 wives!), but since monogamy was introduced in the nineteenth century by the British Imperialists, having multiple wives became illegal in many parts of India. Yet in the Muslim world, it is often legal. Until the Marriage Act of 1953, the ideal household in China consisted of "one man, many wives, and as many children as possible" (Gu, 1922; Xia et al., 2003). In Japan, polygamy was declared illegal only after the country was defeated in World War II and occupied by the U.S. army. But I will stop here and turn to more important facts.

Whatever the state of law is today, in China, Korea, Japan, and South-East Asia in general, a gentleman can only have one legal wife, but as many concubines, handmaids, or mistresses as he can afford (Gu, 1922). That said, promiscuous young women, even if married, as long as they do not have children, are usually 'available' to powerful men, married or not (Pan, 2004). In fact, there is a wealth of data suggesting that a high proportion of Chinese men are utilizing the increased access to mistresses and prostitutes (Pan, 2004) much more often than men living in the USA (Laumann et al., 1994), where married men tend to turn away from the competition for sexual partners, engage in parental activities, and thus stick to one woman (Gray, Yang & Harrison, 2006). Now, this open attitude towards concubines, handmaids, and mistresses is so omnipresent in Asia (especially in Thailand, Vietnam, China, Japan etc.) that it usually 'blows' the average American or European mind:

> *The Chinese feminine ideal is for a wife to live absolutely, selflessly for her husband. Therefore when a husband who is sick or invalided from overwork requires a handmaid, a hand rack or eye rack [sic] to enable him to get well and to make him fit for his life work, the wife in China with her selflessness gives it to him just as a good wife in Europe and America gives an armchair or goat's milk to her husband when he is sick or requires it.* (Gu Hongming, 1922)

When the West implemented its imperial agenda, like in all historical conquest, naturally the conqueror turned to the females of the conquered. What happened after this encounter with Asian sexuality, especially during the last 150 years of Western hegemony, can only be described as the thorough construction of a fabulous, sexist 'Asian exoticism.' This exoticism, in my view, demotes the submissive Asian woman to a plaything, and puts her at the mercy of Western master-race dominance. Asia thus became 'feminized':

"I shall choose a little yellow-skinned woman with black hair and cat's eyes. She must be pretty. Not much bigger than a doll..."

...are the words of Louis Marie-Julien Viaud (1850-1923), alias Pierre Loti, an officer in the French navy stationed in Nagasaki, in his book *Madame Chrysantheme* (1887). The book talks about short-term marriages with Japanese 'rashamen' or "concubines of Westerners" (Loti, 2001).

This kind of representation of Asian woman and Asian sexuality prevails in hundreds of artworks, books, films, television shows, and musicals, and almost always entails interracial romances between European or American men with Asian women, for example in John Luther Long's *Madame Butterfly* (Long, 2002), John Paris' *Kimono* (Paris, 1947), Arthur Golden's *Memoirs of a Geisha* (Golden, 1997), Max Clavell's *Shogun* and *Tai-pan* (Clavell, 1986), and, of course, Marguerite Duras' notorious *L'Amant*, in which a French teenage girl becomes the submissive, Sinicized mistress of a much older Chinese gentleman (Duras, 1984). And I haven't even mentioned more hedonistic works such as Wei Hui's *Shanghai Baby* (Wei, 2002) or Chun Sue's *Beijing Doll* (Chun, 2004).

As Patricia Lin argued in *Invented Asia* (2007), "sexual encounters historically were initially predominantly between Western white men and Asian woman given the nature of colonial and business ventures which tended to favor situations where primarily men were sent out into Asian territories." This is testified by the fact that Chinese and Japanese writers found it natural to depict dominant Western men as 洋鬼子 (yang guizi, foreign devils from the ocean), who were evil, stout, and ugly (Zhou, 2000).

What happened in Asia before and between the First and Second Opium Wars (1839-1842; 1856-1860), the World Wars (1914-1918; 1938-1945), the Korean War (1950-1953), the occupation of Japan (1945-1952), Vietnam (1959-1975), and during the U.S. hegemony in Japan (1945-) compelled Western mass media and cultural consumer entertainment to strengthen the objectification of Asia: Asia as an all-perverted – animalistic if you like – place of Western sexual dominance versus Asian sexual submission:

The most obvious use of the postwar American discourse about Japanese 'feudalism' in justifying the U.S. occupation was to render the Japanese as helpless and naïve as women and children supposedly were. (Naoko Shibusawa, 2006)

Butterflies, amber, pottery, calligraphy, lotus flowers, cherry trees, dolls, silk, kimonos... are those national symbols of a masculine or feminine nature? Westerners found them to be of a feminine nature, and commented on the absence of more manly sports (soccer, football, baseball, basketball, athletics etc.), and the toy-like houses and cities they encountered. They started a "discourse of femininity and masculinity, or femininity and maturity merged, male activity and female passivity," or simply about "race and manliness" (Shibusawa, 2006).

However, no such discourse took place in Germany, which was defeated in World War I and World War II. Perhaps this was because Germany's population was predominantly white and Western. At the heart of Europe, Germany was considered to be a grown-up culture comparable to the Anglo-American one; by all means the Germans were "a mature people" (Douglas McArthur, in Shibusawa, 2006).

Not only gender and maturity, but also such concepts as 'love' and 'privacy' were believed to be of an altogether different nature in Asia. In Korea, Indonesia, Singapore, Thailand, Vietnam, China, and India it is still the case, even a decade or two into this new millennium, that most marriages are arranged or 'match-made,' and that 'marriage' is still considered the 'union of two families' rather than of two individuals, and that a man has to marry and have a child, preferably a boy, before he is considered a real 'man.' Nevertheless, we should bear in mind that today's situation in those countries is already a huge improvement over what it was 20 to 30 years ago (Lü, 2005). Some Western authors still argue that 'Love has nothing to do with marriage in Asia' (Nilson, 1988). Or, in defense of Asian values, that the concept of 'love' in (Confucian) China, Japan, and *tutti quanti* is inherently different from that in Christianity and the West, and can and must be understood 'in the Asian context' only (Lin, 2007).

Similarly, in Asia's collective societies, the concept of 'privacy' must be understood 'in that Asian context' only (McDougall, 2002). It might be helpful to keep this rule in mind: In China, 'love' and 'privacy' are best expressed by 爱 (ai) and 私 (si). Korean and Japanese speakers can read and understand these two characters, but pronounce them differently and also transliterate them into their own alphabets, Hangul and Hiragana, respectively. The concept of individual 'privacy' which we take for granted in the West was imported into Hangul and Katakana simply because there was no generic word for it in classical Korean and Japanese. Linguistic distance correlates with cultural distance – only if one has gone through the painful ordeal of mastering a foreign language will one understand and appreciate a foreign culture and its distinctive values.

Some feminists (men can also be great feminists) have argued that the whole image of 'Asian playthings' is the construct of an obsessive Western mind. But then, so are the stock market and French cuisine. No idea that has occupied so many minds over hundreds of years can be that far away from the facts of human life.

Unless someone speaks a foreign language fluently and is familiar with the cultural implications of certain words and expressions, one is unlikely to understand the cultural context of, let's say, 'enjo kosai' in Japan – a compensated dating of young schoolgirls by middle-aged men (Goldman, 2008/05) – modern concubinage in Hong Kong or Shanghai, or rampant prostitution in most East Asian countries. Similarly, an East Asian person will have difficulty understanding European 'swinger culture,' where couples exchange their sex partners, even wives, mixed saunas, or the naturist or 'nudist culture' valued in many European societies.

But it isn't all relative: In the past it has always been the Western male colonialist or imperialist who came to Asia, not the Eastern male colonialist or imperialist who came to Europe. Where women dress like dolls, are submissive, know that their husbands will cheat anyway, where prostitution is cheap, people are beautiful, slim, young, even easy to marry, where languages are unreadable, and where Asian body types, in particular exotic Asian facial features, skin color, and genital configurations seem to arouse Western men to the very heights of exoticism and bizarreness (Lin, 2007), there will be a market for it:

> *I have met the plaything which I have, vaguely perhaps, desired all my life: a little talking cat. [...] her head, the size of your first, is poised, and seems unreal, on a child's neck, a neck too long and too thin; and her tiny nothingness of a body is lost in the folds of an extravagant dress, hugely flowered with great gilded chrysanthemums.*
> (Pierre Loti, 2001)

Dominant groups, therefore, are able to transmit their ideologies and sexual categories through powerful cultural means of subjugation.

Just as Asia had to bend down and suffer under Western military and economic might, so did it have to be submissive to the 'dominance vs. submission' sexuality catechism. As long as those occupied cultures did not become 'Westernized,' i.e. did not conform to a certain level of moral conduct set by Europe and the USA, they remained "stripped of all privileges and left with an ascribed eroticism that invites sexual engagement, exploitation and ultimate abandonment" (Lin, 2007).

Now, while all the authors and scholars quoted above allude to the 'animal instinct' of bad Western wolves and innocent Asian sheep, I cannot quite get myself to agree with these 'chronicles of victimization' of Asia that only play further into the hands of Western dominance. On the contrary, I do believe that in our modern world, civility will prevail over barbarism. Or, as one of China's major entertainers, Jackie Chan, alias Cheng Long [成龙], once said, "We urge more foreigners to marry Chinese women!"

Well, Mr. Chan, this is what Western men usually do in China. Or, at least that is what they aspire to do, not only in China, but in the whole of East Asia. To put this into socioeconomic perspective: In an international world, Ms. Asia has already claimed Ms. West's boyfriend. Ms. Asia will make sure that her culture prevails, and, believe it or not, he will spend his money on her and, facing the shortage of children and crisis back home, he will stake his future on her and her kin.

On a philosophical level, the idea of a masculine West and a feminine East that transcends all human experience and forms a sense of liberation and harmony – Blaise Pascal called it *logique du Coeur*, or 'wisdom of the heart' – is a popular concept of dualism, also evident in yin and yang (阴阳): the feminine or negative principle in nature, or moon, and the masculine or positive principle in nature, or sun.

Jim Garrison, in his *Civilization and the Transformation of Power*, took this duality to the most profound level when he analyzed today's gender politics using folk wisdom and mythology (Garrison, 2000). He describes how the suppression of 'Mother Earth,' the archetypal feminine, has led us to the brink of world catastrophe, heralded by the 'Crisis of Europe' in works such as Donella Meadows' *The Limits to Growth* (1972), Oswald Spengler's *The Decline of the West* (1893), and Edmund Husserl's *The Crisis of the European Sciences* (1970). The power plays between 'Mother mind' and 'Father force,' the violent tension between 'Mahimata' (Mother Earth) and Lord Shiva (god of destruction) – all cultures have their myths about this duality and can follow its discourse:

Here – the destructive power of the short-sighted masculine West that narrow-mindlessly focuses on objects, not relations, and that wants to exploit and manipulate those objects in order to control nature and all things.

There – the gentle power of the long-sighted feminine East that holistically perceives the world's interconnectedness of all objects, and that cultivates and appreciates them in order to balance the relations among all things.

The Dialectics of Dichotomy

Having seen that the East-West dichotomy is omnipresent in history, philosophy, demographics, religion, culture, ideology, even sexuality, let us now, in looking at the dialectics of dichotomy, expand its scope to more exotic fields such as physiology, geopolitics, and cognition:

1) *Cerebral Determinism*

This notion is linked to human physiology.

We observe, in most cultures, the grammatical division of nouns into masculine and feminine, and in all cultures, the semantic division of names and objects into male and female. It means that gender is an innate sense people have of themselves and others, including animals and objects. This is an example of our human physiology, the structure of our sexes, correctly corresponding to and portraying categorizations of things in the world we perceive. Next, we all are able to distinguish between matter and idea. In philosophy this is called Cartesian dualism (*Cambridge Dictionary*, 1999), which is an example of the intimate relationship between our mind and brain correctly corresponding and portraying categorizations of mind and matter in the world we perceive. Likewise, the ways we think about the world we perceive with respect to our categorizations of matter and idea are causally determined or influenced by our linguistic system (Sapir, 1983). Since our physiology projects itself onto the world we perceive, this makes me wonder whether our definition of an inductive East and an analytical West is another example of the structure of our cognitive system – the two cerebral hemispheres – correctly corresponding and portraying categorizations of the world we perceive. The East-West dichotomy is not an invention; it is a discovery.

2) *The Theory of Shared Labor*

The second notion I would like to bring forward is the argument of shared labor in a geopolitical context, not in a Marxist or Weberian sense to explain labor shared within a society, but to explain labor shared among civilizations.

The definition of the East-West dichotomy (from Greek *dicha*, 'apart,' and *tomos* 'cutting') is a form of logical division consisting of the separation of the geopolitical map into two hemispheres, one of which has and the other has not in each case perpetually exhibited the tendency for analytically-based reasoning or integration-based reasoning. In any population, just as we may divide its members along a vertical scale into professional individuals and individuals who are not professionals (and each of these may be subdivided again), similarly we may divide cultures along a horizontal scale into analytically-based societies and societies which are integration-based. Because each side has what the other side is lacking, East and West together form a whole that is imperfect without both of its parts. If we now come to see the division into integration-based and analytically-based civilizations as a form of specialization in 'cooperative labor' with specific tasks and roles well adjusted to increase efficiency and intellectual output of humankind, we could imagine a certain regulatory mechanism or 'collective consciousness' that shifts whole populations – voluntary or involuntary – into their respective geopolitical roles and provides them with specific tasks so as to serve the greater good of the whole.

Ideas about a human 'hive mind' are not new to us. However, comparing insect and human societies still causes confusion (Cooley & Rieff, 1983; 2003). Not too long after Darwin observed group strategies and social organization in animals in his *Origin of Species* (1859), modern biologists and sociologists compared ant kingdoms (and occasionally, beehives) to human state-building and consumerism (Spencer, 1857; Hölldobler & Wilson, 1990, 1994; Weber, 1991; Marion, 1999). Philosophers tell us that there is a certain unifying moral force within society; psychologists talk about 'conformity' or 'group identification' as opposed to a society of total egoists and independent individuals (Cooley & Rieff, 1983). If this holds true for groups, why not for civilizations? In order to be most productive and efficient, labor must be shared.

To my knowledge, no Western culture has ever produced anything like the works of Confucius, and no Eastern culture has ever produced anything like Plato's ideas. The notion of shared labor makes me think that the division into an analytically-based

West and an integration-based East could be no coincidence in human evolution, but a collective behavior to fully exploit and develop all the cognitive capacities of the human race. Note that there is nothing in this world that is not shared by all humankind. It is just that the West grew up to excel in this, and the East grew up to excel in that. We must only combine them in order to express all the knowledge.

3) Cognitive Dualism

The third notion is derived from John Dewey (1859-1952). In his book *The Quest for Certainty* (1929) he discusses the 'doctrine of two truths,' the sacred and the profane, which in turn is derived from dualism.

Dualism, in its simplest notion, is related to binary thinking, that is, to systems of thought that are two-valued: valid/invalid, true/false, good/bad, right/wrong. The doctrine of two truths, however, is more concretely used in the dualistic response to the conflict between spiritualism and science, the spiritual and the secular. Dewey saw all philosophical problems as being derived from dualistic oppositions, in particular between the spirit and physical matter, but it is his conclusion that is most significant: Dewey advocated rejecting Hegel's dialectical idealism (that recommended the synthesis of oppositions seen as theses versus antitheses) on the grounds that the whole (synthesis) is never the sum of its parts (thesis and antithesis). Conclusively, contradictions are universal: It is 'either-or' or 'both but incommensurable,' as for example 'ebb and flow,' 'yin and yang,' or as the Chinese-English saying goes: "鱼和熊掌，不可兼得" ("You can't have your cake and eat it, too" – unabridged: "鱼,我所欲也；熊掌，亦我所欲也，二者不可得兼，舍鱼儿取熊掌者也" [Mencius, 11A, 4]).

The study of the 'other,' Jean-Paul Sartre's xenophobic masochism as expressed in "l'enfer, c'est les autres," Jürgen Habermas' paranoid 'der Blick des anderen,' or the Indian philosophy of 'Deshi-Pardeshi' (Inhabitor vs. Outsider), the silly but deadly communist-capitalist game – all of these simply indicate: I am not you, and you are not me. So, what is the argument? Don't we all like to disagree, not because we have the better reasons, but because we can disagree? Isn't it our right to say that "although 'your' country is made of gold, 'I' don't like it!" Don't I have the right to say no? It was in structuralism, famously represented by Claude Lévi-Strauss, where one did not only organize human thought and culture into binary oppositions, but attached hierarchies to them as well. For some reason in the European history of ideas, 'rational' is usually privileged and associated with men, while 'emotional' is inferior and associated with women. Blond hair in Western culture is privileged and associated with goodness, while black hair is inferior and associated with evil, and so on (Boon, 1972; Goddard, 1982). Was Lévi-Strauss right if one wanted to say that the 'West' is privileged and associated with 'mastering the theories,' while the 'East' is inferior and associated with 'mastering the arts'? Surely, cultural values and prejudices vary over time. What does not is the underlying, psychologically calibrated mechanism of all human reasoning: its cognitive dualism.

To sum up, the above three notions demonstrate what seems to be a law of nature, namely that the East-West difference has been found consistently from the time of the Greeks 2,500 years ago to our present day, and that it is consistent with assumptions about our anatomy, the cerebral hemispheres, the dual nature of our reasoning, and the geopolitical concept of sharing labor (by way of collective consciousness) for the greater good and a higher efficiency in intellectual output. Because the human geopolitical situation is a mere extension of the physical and cognitive systems inherent in each of us, we have reason to believe that our societies, our planetary civilization, will continue to be predominantly dualistic in the near future, with an integration-based Eastern hemisphere and an analytically-based Western hemisphere.

Problems with the Dichotomy

There are a few problems with the East-West dichotomy as a global theory that need to be addressed in order to allow further discussion and research. Of all criticisms, these are the urgent ones I shall comment on:

1) *Generalizations*

The biggest accusation by scholars is that of 'generalizations': 'East' and 'West,' these two categories, so we are told, are oversimplifying the current world order and all other cultural, geographical, historical, political, and social affairs (Hendry, 2006).

We oppose the argument by saying that 'East and West' indeed contain all those subcategories, and many more. However, every one of them is true only in the abstract, widest, most universal sense of the word, and any definition is subject to change. For example, we have explicitly concluded that the West is more deductive, while the East is more inductive. In that way, generalizations pose no harm to scholarship, which distinguishes between Western philosophy and Eastern philosophy departments. Besides, 'East and West' as an interdisciplinary concept has been the rough guide for universal historians such as Hannah Arendt (1993), Arnold Toynbee (1958), Tu Weiming (2003), Joseph Needham (1964), Kitaro Nishida (1989), Okakura Kakuzo (1904), and Ji Xianlin (2006), as well as for universal theoreticians such as Francis Bacon (1620), Thomas Hobbes (1671), Friedrich Nietzsche (1909), Karl Marx (1848), Samuel Huntington (1993), and hundreds more. They all did research on the conceptual contrast between Eastern and Western societies and, either directly or indirectly, came (often independently from each other) to the conclusion that there are two cultural modes of humankind: the more rational, deduction-driven West, and the more intuitive, induction-driven East. This is simply how things are.

Still, the East-West dichotomy is occasionally misunderstood by prominent individuals or special interest groups who do not like to be categorized, which is understandable. Yet, again, its aim is not to label individuals, but to describe entire civilizations and their cultural evolution, an evolution that is very real (Mace, 2005; Reynolds, 1983; Cavalli-Sforza et al., 1994).

Moreover, the branch of social science that effectively uses empirical investigation and critical analysis to understand the structure of Eastern and Western societies, 'Sociology' or 'Sociology of Cultures,' usually observes developments on the macro level of societies, for example: group behavior, social networking, and so on, and never attempts to explain individual activity and behavior. The East-West dichotomy is a global theory, not a local one; and caution is advised when following the recent hype about and around the application of the word *glocal*, meaning global ideas implemented on a local level.

Individuals occasionally feel victimized by scientific studies, and sometimes wronged by anthropological or social scientific findings. Yet we need to remind ourselves that categorization, and therefore a degree of oversimplification and generalization, are inherent in our everyday lives. Individuals as well as small groups are categorized by school grades, credit systems, occupation, profession, social status, ethnicity, even by the clothes we wear, the quarters we live in, the car we drive, and the books we read. In the case of East and West we are talking about the cultural evolution, specification, and stratification of ideas of civilizations over the last 2,500 years and earlier, with billions of very diverse individuals and their various actions filling up empty time with living history.

If zooming into separate households, naturally we would find each individual of that household having many identities. They identify themselves, for example, by their faith, profession, social status, ethnicity, hobbies, friends etc.

Looking at humankind from the moon, however, those identities can be ascribed to a certain region, cultural group, and civilization, East or West. Therefore, no individual today, no group of individuals should be offended, or – depending on their point of view – disappointed if they cannot see themselves fitting neatly into the universal categories of East or West. It is a universal theory, not the story of any individual.

2) Stereotypes

A cold-blooded scientist would – in the words of Oscar Wilde – "know the price of everything but the value of nothing." It is a stereotype, and a bit cynical perhaps, to pitch a trained scientist against the notion of God, faith, human feelings, value statements, and spiritual or charitable affairs. A scientist who describes God, poetry, music, or our love for children using statistical models is – you will forgive me for saying so – not an affable companion. But the scientist armed with his methods and measuring tools is also limited by them, and can often only speak about his branch of knowledge and the scientific community. There are other important seekers of truth: the artist, the poet, the philosopher, the musician, the sage, the father and the mother. They all have slightly different approaches to knowledge and wisdom and see things differently from the scientist because they have gleaned their knowledge from personal experiences, learning, practice, or through poetry, music, exercise, or the love of children. We could say then that any activity leads to categorization, and any categorization may result in stereotyping.

The art of stereotyping in cultural studies, like all taxonomies, helps us to make sense of the world around us and to attribute to various groups of people certain characteristics that sum up our experiences and our knowledge about them. That also makes stereotypes very flexible, since they change after our experiences and our knowledge about them has been modified. Therefore, no stereotype can exist that does not have at least some reference point to the factual world, to gathered information, or to personal experiences with a foreign culture. Stereotypes are inevitable. The only danger, as some observers have pointed out, is when they are negative, unfair, politically incorrect (we come to that in a minute) or too inflexible. This is because stereotypes, like all beliefs, have the tendency to become stronger over time, and, when constantly repeated by propaganda, can be used to manipulate uninformed public opinion to connect people or events that were originally unrelated:

> *The self-fulfilling prophecy is, in the beginning, a false definition of a situation evoking new behavior, which makes the original false conception come 'true.' This specious validity of the self-fulfilling prophecy perpetuates a reign of error. For the prophet will cite the actual course of events as proof that he was right from the very beginning.*
> (Robert K. Merton, 1968)

In other words, there is the theoretical possibility that the East-West stereotypes, as natural as they appear today, have become true only because so many people have acted upon and believed in them for thousands of years.

3) Small Nations and Peripheral Nations

Both cultural hemispheres, East and West, are divided into many more distinct societies. And those societies are subdivided into distinct regions. As said elsewhere here, looking at the trees or leaves will divert one's attention from seeing the whole forest. For that reason, it seems unnecessary to discuss each and every society or region and their peculiarities. It is their cultural, economical, and political affiliation, shared history and values, and general relationship that give them a distinct culture, without discussing the charms of each independent member community.

Having said that, I don't need to elaborate on the role of the peripheral regions: The Middle East, Africa, Australia, and Latin America all have close cultural, economical, and political affiliations, shared history and values, and a general relationship with either Europe or Asia, or both on equal terms, in which case the relationship may be balanced for a while or else eventually turn in favor of one side or the other.

As for the relationships between large states and small states within the cultural hemispheres, they may at times perceive themselves as independent, even smaller states which are obviously less powerful and more dependent but nevertheless feel they are special and unique. In addition, all nations by definition insist on their sovereignty or exclusivity. But all the same, together, those large countries and small countries are interdependent and form civilizations.

Returning to the world of politics, one could say there is no such thing as absolute independence and liberty, not for any state, not for any group of people. The French moralist Joseph Joubert (1754-1824), who experienced the French Revolution, called any noble cry for liberty a farce:

Let your cry be for free souls rather even than for free men. [...] Subordination is in itself a better thing than independence. The one implies order and arrangement; the other implies only self-sufficiency with isolation. The one means harmony, the other a single tone; the one is the whole, the other is but the part. (Jospeh Joubert, 1962)

We could ask: What if one part of the whole *fails* to participate in or commit or contribute to its social environment? I would argue that in that case, if a small, solitary state tries to single-mindedly change the pattern of the whole empire, it can only do so within the limits set by all other neighboring states. Within the global community of nations, each of its smaller members will be ruthlessly assessed, persistently judged for its performance, and punished if it misbehaves or fails to perform:

今也小国师大国，而耻受命焉；是有犹弟子而耻受命于先师也。如耻之，莫若师文王；师文王，大国五年，小国七年，必为政于天下矣。

Now, the small states imitate the large, and yet are ashamed to receive their commands: This is like a scholar's being ashamed to receive the commands of his master. If the small states know their place, they will benefit from the greatness of their masters. (Mencius, 7A, 3)

4) Political Correctness

Some great negotiators, like former United Nations Secretary Kofi Annan, or now his successor, the South Korean Ban Ki-moon, would not approve of dividing the world into two cultural hemispheres, or at least they would shy away from this for the reasons given above. Generalizations, stereotypes, and categorizations lead to separatism and isolation, to nationalism, prejudice, and even racism. In short, all these would be bad for the United Nations' good governance and true scholarship.

The fear of new totalities in itself is not so new. But if Eastern and Western values, mutual respect, balance, harmony, and the difficulties that we face if the West continues down its aggressive path are not addressed, I would argue that even without mentioning the concept of the East-West dichotomy, there are still going to be the dangers of separatism and isolation, nationalism, and other factors that are detrimental to good governance and true scholarship.

Since everyone in world politics seems so concerned about the price we have to pay for the different civilization modes of humankind, we should find a peaceful place to discuss the value of it all. The United Nations, and by inclusion its member states, are committed and have been informed countless times by the universal historians and philosophers, great thinkers, and Nobel laureates in East and West, that there is cultural diversity that not only needs to be addressed again and again (because people sadly tend to forget), but far better *understood*, appreciated, and valued. The Universal Declaration of Human Rights, The Dialogue among Civilizations (Khatami, 2001), The Declaration of Human Responsibilities (Küng, 1997), and so on are cases in point. It is important that all nations recognize and cherish the two great cultural modes in general and the myriads of cultural varieties in particular: the *value* created for the future of mankind by being different, not the price paid in the past for forcing us to conform.

Asian nations are now a majority in number, opinion, and theory; their reviving cultures are now of the greatest political concern to the Western hegemony that still holds sway over the world. Therefore, in the near future it will be inevitable in global affairs to separate political rhetoric from socio-cultural realities, and we should expect more policymakers and historians to talk about 'cultural politics' or 'political culture,' because there isn't just one political or one cultural model – there are many, and what works for one does not necessarily work for another. As mentioned previously, Asia is now a greater phenomenon than the USA or Europe. Unabashed *resistance* to – or worse, outright denial of – Asian values, Eastern philosophies, cultural achievements, and Asia's greater participation in world affairs and its reformation could lead to a clash of civilizations, just like Samuel Huntington had prophesized. The concept of 'political correctness' exists, but so far, there isn't such a thing as *cultural correctness*.

5) Polarities

There is a well-informed block of political analysts and economists who try to convince us that the relationship between Europe's 'Big Three' (Germany, France, Great Britain) plus the USA, and Asia's 'Big Three' (China, India, Japan) plus maybe Russia, is only superficial, toxic, and full of congenital defects (Rosan, 1962; Hendry, 2006). I suggest the alternative to this division between a Western league and an Eastern one would be inevitable chaos: All nation-states would act as separate entities that form alliances at any time with whoever is able or willing, thus arbitrarily leading the world into *unipolarity* (one center of power), *bipolarity* (two centers of power), or *multipolarity* (three or more centers of power), with no such thing as a cultural East-West divide.

Such a theory looks like a deliberately broken glass window to me. Valuable time and energy would be wasted on the analysis of shards. The basic unit of human relationships is 'two.' One cannot have a relationship with nobody. But some people neglect this human aspect of relationships, and collect data and produce statistics about each country's human and non-human capital, resources, and natural endowments instead, which is nothing less than adopting the strictly economic or materialist approach. The social materialists see humans as being more guided by the sciences and natural laws, and less by the humanities, for example Jared Diamond in his *Guns, Germs and Steel* (2003) and Gunnar Heinsohn in his *Söhne und Weltmacht* (2005).

The social materialistic approach is an extension of Marxist materialism, or maybe just another fancy name for bean-counting. This very (Western) analytical, deduction-based approach to make sense of the world and all relationships does not allow for any value, metaphysical discussion, ideologies, and spiritual meaning. It does not acknowledge 'oneness,' 'balance,' or 'harmoniousness,' nor does it allow for human morals or factors like 'tolerance,' 'respect,' 'love,' and 'forgiveness.' It does not let man assume a greater role than being a mere statistic.

It demonstrates once again that particular Western *lack of ideas* and *confusion* I was talking about earlier: the limits of the Western cultural mode and deductive-based science, which in essence were almost begging for the re-emergence of the spiritual East, its former glories, wisdom, and its power to heal the global imbalance.

So, the West still thinks it's all about who's got the oil, who's got the money, who's got the guns, or, better, who's got the biggest guns. That's how our children now think and are trained to reason. If *your* numbers add up, *you* are at the top of the league. This is a conclusion reached via the deductive way. Let us recall: In *deductive reasoning* we reach a conclusion from previously known facts, a conclusion that is sound and valid. That is the tragedy of our cause, and the cause for our decline. We are totally deluded and lost in an artificial world of infinite particulars, of which we do not know how to let go and get out. Religious people, no matter of which faith, who usually strive to become good, lovable, modest, humble, and kind people (in their respective communities) now look like total idiots, when some hedge funds managers, bankers, or lawyers got wealthy and powerful by ruthlessly destroying their competitors, and exploiting their employees and positions in society. Families, communities, and religions are corrupted this way and fall apart.

And this is precisely how some world historians and political analysts see the community of nations falling apart into self-interested economic zones, political spheres of influence, highly specialized manufacturing power bases, and so on: a fragmented, multipolar world with nothing more in common than a materialist drive for fighting over resources, market shares, and political influence. In such a model, the Western model, states may fail like business models fail, like many companies fail. But is this really how we should look at humanity? How can a culture *fail*, if left in peace? How can a civilization *fail*, if not be annihilated?

All the while, the East with its inductive ways simply allocates new relations to recurring phenomenal patterns; it shamelessly makes unscientific yet highly humanistic predictions and acts upon them, like Zhang Zai (1020-1077), who said: "All humans are my brothers and sisters; all things are my companions," and Tu Weiming: "We need to establish a harmonious yet diverse new order of world ethics" (Tu, 2012). Now that the East is rising again, few Westerners are ready to deal with true cultural diversity upon being confronted with thousands of "new" terms, holistic world views, and Eastern thought. It may take some time for most Western scholars to adjust and fully appreciate, let alone pay tribute to and benefit from the South Asian and East Asian traditions: The sole reign of the Western hemisphere is coming to an end.

The East-West dichotomy predicts that if the world were to be reshuffled and recreated, under any circumstances it would happen all over again: the division of humankind into many various cultures that together form two great cultural hemispheres. One would be *more* rational, analytical, and deductive; the other *more* intuitive, spiritual, and inductive. It is an evolutionary program that runs in all of us. It is not arbitrary. It is either-or, in the same way cerebral determinism, cognitive dualism, and shared labor are part of our human nature. The dichotomy doesn't respond to economic or political theories; on the contrary, economic and political theories respond to the dichotomy. That's because first there's humanity, and then come the theories.

According to the East-West dichotomy, there is only *equilibrium*. This equilibrium may never be perfect and, at times, may tilt more to one side than the other. Yet according to this, the world can never be unipolar or multipolar.

6) Incommensurability

If asked about a single, unified humanity, no reasonable person would openly disagree with this possibility. It seems rational: One China plus one Germany makes one...what? The two have different traditions; they are not similar. Humanity should never be subjected to *Gleichschaltung*, a German term which means 'synchronization' or enforced 'conformity,' be it cultural or political co-optation. Humanity really means *all* of us, the entire range of human beings and their diverse cultural and political idiosyncrasies, core values, inventions, and contributions. If we look at it this way, the idea of humanity is a very beautiful and decent thing. It is unbiased and entirely positive. We simply feel we have to be part of that humanity; in fact, our humanity is something we can't escape. Sure, we can always improve ourselves and actively promote the education of better human beings.

So what do people in the international arena say when they talk about humanity? They talk about East and West. Be they presidents, political or business leaders, journalists, or just exchange students or tourists, they all talk about cultural differences, nationalities, countries and their histories, about supposed similarities. Those who deny there are differences are usually those that never studied another culture. At some point, the Westerners in Asia are going to proudly side with the West: "*We* in the West…" or "*they* in the East." How many books have already been written about East and West? Why is it that every Westerner knows about 'East and West,' talks about 'East and West,' belongs to either 'East or West,' and almost anxiously wants to discuss 'East and West'?

Here is a possible explanation: Despite the outrageous disunity of the European nation states and the dysfunctional bureaucracy of the European Union, those 400 million or so citizens do not only embrace a common 'Magna Carta of Liberty' or 'Magna Carta of Democracy and Human Rights,' but also a 'Magna Carta of Loyalty.' What do I mean by 'Magna Carta of Loyalty'? The European powers, after so many centuries of 'jointly conquering and dividing the world,' in the end had nothing else to do than to ditch their territories or else declare war on each other. They were after power, and how to get it. After the two Great Wars that shattered Europe, all of their remaining former colonies became independent. It seems but a rational choice to me that the Europeans should unite once more to jointly face the New World Order, or else get the imperialist payback they truly deserve, especially in the face of the rising powers of the Muslim/Arabic, Indian, and Chinese civilizations.

In fact, if I was non-European, and I wanted to manipulate Europe, I would do my utmost to distract the Europeans from their 'Magna Carta of Loyalty.' I would try to undermine their 'loyalty,' to play them and their interests against each other. Granted, by saying "Magna Carta of Loyalty of the European nations" I mean the European nations' faithfulness to the European cause: the forceful continuation and domination of their civilization by means of their rational, analytically-based ways and deductive cultural mode over all worldly affairs, standards, institutions, politics, economics, and social issues. The European thinkers will desperately try to cling to their *Deutungshoheit*, a German term meaning 'sovereignty over the definition of thought.' It basically means that whatever new knowledge the Europeans believe to have 'discovered' in foreign cultures – indigenous concepts, names, ideas – they almost always *translated* those unique and non-European concepts into familiar, convenient European terms.

Naturally, we are loyal to our common ancestors, heredity, language, and community. It is an evolutionary tactic to ensure the survival and procreation of our kind. That is why Americans, Europeans, and the Commonwealth realm, despite all their internal struggles and disputes, nevertheless refer to themselves as the 'West.' The same applies to the various nation states in Asia that, despite all their internal struggles and disputes, nevertheless refer to themselves as the 'East.'

That is why East and West are incommensurable concepts: Nothing can belong simultaneously to both parts; nor can both parts simultaneously occupy the same space.

The Future of the Dichotomy

In order to balance the East-West dichotomy and engage in meaningful dialogue guided by the principles of peaceful aim, mutual respect, tolerance, and patience, we should discourage any maneuver designed to 'cheat,' 'take over,' 'support hegemony,' and other evil acts by making laws or introducing binding oaths. To this end, unchecked Eurocentrism as well as Asiacentrism should be avoided at all costs.

It seems necessary to address some of those areas that in my view deserve serious attention:

1) Education

Oscar Wilde once said, "Nothing that is worth having can be taught," meaning that everything that is worth having is acquired through experience and self-cultivation, and it has to be acquired willingly: experience for the purpose of experiencing. Those high-profile Western officials, directors, and businessmen who desire to govern, trade, research, or teach, should spend some time in Asian countries, and attend Asian universities or other institutes of higher learning, finance, or trade. This should be made compulsory for any foreign leader in Asia. In fact, no executive, expatriate, leader of a party, director of a large organization, let alone head of state, should be allowed to assume such a post without having spent some time in Asia and learned the local language. Such enlightened 'conditions' are already an unspoken agreement in many scholarly circles and practiced in international law-making, but are far from being the rule in politics and economics. Therefore it should be made mandatory to spend some years abroad, just as a foreign postgraduate qualification should be made mandatory for the highest scholarly posts. No nation, no matter how big, can afford half-educated leaders.

2) Politics

Biology, culture, policies – this is the hierarchy of change. One can change one's biology only through choice of courtship and the result of offspring, but one can slowly change one's culture within one's own lifetime by immigration, marriage, and learning. However, one's policies are the quickest to change.

Policies, nowadays, are the greatest cognitive intrusion of all, as they are the fastest manipulation of memory and information. They are widely recognized as the single most important method to deal with one's 'opponents' effectively. So, what policies are Western politicians carrying out these days? Western politicians have a keen interest in making all Asian cultures and traditions conform to Western civilization, be it through Capitalism, market globalization, democracy, human rights, preemptive wars, sporting events, Santa Claus, or Coca-Cola.

Since globalization and 'World History' as an academic discipline, as mentioned before, are considered extensions of Western civilization and Western history, it is relatively safe for Western politicians, negotiators, and scholars to make concessions (e.g. allowing China to join the World Trade Organization, despite its authoritarian regime), give freebies (e.g. nuclear weapons to India), or occasionally praise, however shallow, all kinds of cultural achievements, be they of the past or present. How all these niceties will add up to substantial Eastern representation in international affairs remains to be seen. First, how does any country know if it is 'in' if there is no 'out' in globalism? Second, who will take credit for what comes out of Asia's input? Will it be the West?

When Francis Bacon first finished his *Novum Organum* (*The New Instrument*) in 1620, he originally had Aristotle's *Organum* in mind and quoted only a few of China's great inventions like printing and gunpowder. However, after hearing about the Four Books of Confucianism, and especially after reading Confucius' *Great Learning* (*Da Xue*, 大学), is it mere coincidence that Bacon thereupon included his *Novum Organum* in a six-volume masterpiece which he proudly titled *The Great Renewal of Learning*?

All world governments know the hierarchy of change: biological – cultural – policy changes. Because Western governments are short-lived (and thus, for the pragmatic reason of survival, politically short-sighted), they will focus all their energies and efforts on new policies, *short-time* changes, to prove what they can do for the moment. Meanwhile, they ignore the long-term effects on the culture as a whole. Eastern governments are different: They still keep an eye on cultural, long-term changes and maintenance. If a government would openly endorse a strategy for biological change, this could lead – as it did in the past – to suspicions of xenophobia, racism, and isolation, so biological changes are the ones best not overtly promoted by any government.

If we were to improve international cooperation, Eastern and Western policymakers, scientists, and economists would have to create shared opportunities for growth, consistent with broadly accepted economic theories, open markets, and good diplomacy. The real problem with fast policy changes is that, if one studies history carefully, one will see that violence must follow. In policy-making, 'might is right,' 'whoever controls the stick controls the buffalo,' and 'small countries have no politics.' It is cruel, but this is simply how things are. It is very likely that a powerful person or group might abuse their power through the means of *ad-hoc* policy changes that are very arbitrary, egoistic, and because of their dubious nature, often non-negotiable.

Who was it who said that "the destructive energies of the deduction-based warrior culture would be channeled into the safer pursuits of a commercial society"? Thomas Hobbes, Adam

Smith, Dugald Stewart... another enlightened Scot? That is why we frequently use words like *war* in economics, e.g. trade 'wars,' and *fight* in politics, e.g. 'fighting' for voters.

In policy-making, the West has to relinquish some power, keep its often arbitrary, short-sighted, *ad-hoc* adjustments more in check, and discuss more frequently with its partners on an equal level. At the same time, the East should try harder to be less passive and conservative and more forceful in policy decision-making, otherwise it will always be bullied around by its more pro-active Western counterpart(s).

3) Exchange

Among all things that are tradable – oil, wood, gold, commodities, human capital etc. – culture is the least obvious yet the most subversive good. Since the Orient and Occident produced lots of sustainable, lasting cultural artifacts, arts, ideas, and theories, believe it or not, all these have been the objects of cultural exchange and learning even long before the Greek philosopher Plato *borrowed* some ideas from the Persian sage Zarathustra (who lived c. 600 BC), Alexander the Great's conquest (326 BC-323 BC), and Megasthenes' visit to

Pataliputra (c. 300 BC). Why cultural exchange? Because, for some reason, Alexander thought it worthwhile to risk his reputation, even his empire, by marrying the Bactrian princess Roxane (of today's Northern Afghanistan) in exchange for gold, unity, and political stability. What is more, Megasthenes brought maps and descriptions back to Macedonia in order to inform the Mediterranean world about 'Indica.' And Plato, partly inspired by Persian thought, laid the foundation for Western moral philosophy.

Oh, some may scoff, it was always about trade. That's why human societies expand. Others may say it was about rule and conquest. Human curiosity must have played its part, too. So perhaps did love, on Alexander and Roxane's part. Translation certainly did help to communicate, but did it really help to understand each other? Universally, the first impression upon meeting other cultures is that of amazement and joy, not of fear and anger. It is in the human nature to practice cultural exchange.

So, did this activity of cultural exchange, metaphorically speaking, make the world 'flat' just as Thomas Friedman argued in his bestseller about the effects of globalization and economic exchange? Almost certainly not. On the contrary, cultural exchange, like economics, may benefit both partners, but it does so in entirely different ways. The fundamental psychology beneath all economic activity is the often astonishing fact that one person thinks that a television set is worth more than the 500 Euros he has to pay for it, while the other person thinks that the 500 Euros are worth more than the television set and thus is happy to sell it.

The really fascinating fact, however, is that a society in which everyone sells identical television sets to each other is not sustainable, nor would anyone make any profit. People have to come up with new ideas and inventions every now and then. Coming back from this analogy, East and West will never exchange the same commodities, nor the same cultural goods, nor attach the same value to them. If culture is a market, it is infinite. And unlike money as currency in economics, the currency in cultural exchange is knowledge, not only about facts, but about relationships between facts, between us and them, and between all people and things under heaven.

A culture includes certain religious practices, places of worship, music, festivals, rituals, customs, values, food, clothing, monuments, architecture, language, and arts. The two cultures of East and West, in fact, will not and cannot entirely overlap, because what they have to give is not what they want to take for the same.

4) Translation

Some have argued that we need a 'global language,' and that in today's world, it should be English. For my part, I believe that the proponents of English as a *lingua franca* are crazy, because that is exactly what the Germans once did; now it's the Anglo-Americans who close their 'History' book and say, "We already know you." No, the true 'global language' would be radically different from today's English (or any other major language); it would need to adopt the originality and the tens of thousands of words provided by humankind's other language traditions on top of it.

Every language learner experiences this from time to time: a subconscious certainty that something is lost in translation, every time, without exception. The vocabularies of the world's languages add up, they don't overlap. Translation is something else.

5) World Affairs

The idea that Eastern and Western societies should do everything together because they're exactly the same and their interests are identical is not, as some would have it, a sign of evolutionary maturity or scientific insight, but a desperate form of political manipulation, new Western imperialism, and, yes, wishful thinking. Surely our cultural differences and identities make the world more colorful.

The belief that Eastern and Western societies have the same interests and desires, beliefs and aims, world views, and sense of history seems to me to be an odd mixture of Western insecurity, a desire for *Gleichschaltung* (controlling the hearts and minds of Eastern people via Western-controlled media propaganda, e.g. *The Economist*, British Broadcasting Corporation (BBC), American Cable News Network (CNN), *Times*, Hollywood, international standards etc.), and outright narcissism: "If you want McDonald's and Volkswagen, if you want trade with us, that means – or proves – you *have to be* the same as us."

Aggressive Westernization thus equals a dehumanization of the world community. Ideally, in this world we should maintain two modes of civilization, two forces that counter-check each other, two voices and two choices, *this* and *that* – in other words, we always should be presented with an alternative view. Otherwise, we are left with only one way of reasoning, Western reasoning, that labors under the illusion of possessing the single, absolute, and finite truth. It would lead to a monopoly on 'civilization' as we have seen in the Age of Western imperialism, without respect for tolerance or harmony.

How do East and West engage in a mutually beneficial relationship? If they do engage in one, what form should that relationship take? A communion maybe? And what are the dangers? Maurice Blanchot, a key writer in the twentieth century, expressed this beautifully:

Wherever two entities temporarily evolve into a communion, to be made for each other or not, an engine of war is being built this way. [...] such a communion bears the potential threat of universal destruction.
(Maurice Blanchot, 1983)

If two entities are forced to evolve into a single 'one,' conflict and disaster are inevitable. For all we know, such a union can work forever. But chances are it will end in a terrible fight, terror, and humiliation, just like an arranged marriage that was not to be. If communion fails, if we are left with only one single dominant mode of civilization, it will be a totality.

Regardless of how the universe really is, there is no hope in human affairs for the existence of a single truth; in secular as well as in religious affairs it all comes down to what we truly believe (and want to believe) and how we react towards the 'other.' If there were only two beings left on Earth, no communion would be called for. The two could coexist happily, at a distance. If it is communion that is not meant to be because of the incommensurability of the two great cultural hemispheres and their distinctive ways, I say don't risk it because mutual destruction could follow. Totalities have done us no good. From within itself no civilization offers universal truth. Forced and complete Westernization of humankind, just like its mother and father, colonialism and imperialism, will not only stand trial to the senseless dehumanization of history, it might also create the deadliest potential for mutual self-destruction and loss of morals the world has ever experienced.

Can the West peacefully align itself with the intuitive Eastern powers and thus guarantee all of us a peaceful, fair, and tolerant equilibrium? I say only if the East emancipates itself from the sorry role of a victim of world history. *Now* is the time to become more assertive, *now* is the moment to make reasonable demands. A more powerful Association of Southeast Asian Nations (including Taiwan, Japan, South Korea) is a possibility; the dissolution of the imbalanced 'Group of Eight' (G8) in favor of a new and enlarged 'Group of Twenty' (G20) is another. A lot remains to be done in both hemispheres before they can finally focus their complete attention on each other. There are the peripheral nations of divided Africa, there is Latin America, there is fragile Eastern Europe, and there are the U.S.-led occupation of the Middle East and a military buildup against Europe's greatest ancient foe: the Persians (now Iranians). Plenty of cultural assimilation is going on, unifications by trade and stealth are looming, and lots of pawns are waiting to be moved across the great board of geopolitics.

Without doubt, all cultures and nations have contributed, one way or another, to the overall diversity of human civilization. Yet it is also obvious that some cultures and nations, depending on their antiquity, size, and influence, did contribute *more* than others in the past and, more importantly, will continue to contribute *more* than others in the future. Many will just simply vanish. It is believed that the number of classical Greek and Latin manuscripts combined, an estimated 30,000, is outnumbered by over one million ancient Sanskrit manuscripts that have already been discovered (Taylor, 2008), not to mention millions of Chinese texts written in the Middle Kingdom. However, most Europeans do not want to hear the truth: that they have just been lucky by punching above their weight for too long a time. Economic and cultural activities in themselves are not inventions that are protected by Western patents, nor is the art of statecraft or, for that matter, the art of war.

The Author

THORSTEN PATTBERG, D.Litt. is a scholar at the Institute for Advanced Humanistic Studies at Peking University. He received his Doctor of Letters in Comparative Studies and World Literature from Peking University.

Pattberg was born in Hamm, Germany, in 1977. He grew up in North Rhine-Westphalia, worked as an office clerk at the district court house, and later obtained his master's degree in Asian Studies from the University of Edinburgh, Scotland. He was a Foreign Researcher in the Historiographical Institute at the University of Tokyo, and a Research Fellow in the Sanskrit Department at Harvard University. In China he studied under the guidance of Ji Xianlin, Gu Zhengkun, and Tu Weiming, whom he considers his spiritual masters.

He has published four monographs and more than 20 articles on Comparative Studies that have been published in *China Daily*, *Global Times*, *Shanghai Daily*, *Asia Times*, *German Times*, *Japan Times*, *Korea Herald*, *China Today*, and *Global Research*. His monographs are *The East-West Dichotomy*, *Shengren*, *Holy Confucius*, and *Inside Peking University*. Pattberg also wrote the essays "Language Imperialism – 'Democracy' in China," "Long into the West's Dragon Business," "Chinese Concepts Lost in Translation," and "The End of Translation."

The views expressed in this work are solely those of the author and do not necessarily reflect the views or policies of the above-mentioned institutions.

References

Abe, Masao (1988), "Nishida's Philosophy of 'Place,'" *International Philosophical Quarterly*, No. 28, pp. 355-371.
Abelson, Peter (1993), "Schopenhauer and Buddhism," *East and West*, Vol. 43, No. 2, pp. 255-278.
Abu-Lughod, Janet (1989), *Before European Hegemony: The World System 1250-1350*, Oxford University Press, New York.
Albrecht, Michael (1985), ed., *Oratio de Sinarum philosophia practica: lat.-dt., Rede über die praktische Philosophie der Chinesen* by Christian Wolff, Felix Meiner, Hamburg.
Amnesty International (2005), *Amnesty International Report 2005*. Web. Sept. 2009. <www.amnesty.org>.
An, Yanming (2006), "The Idea of Cheng (Sincerity and Reality) in the History of Chinese Philosophy," *Global Scholarly Publications*. Web. Sept. 2009. <www.gsp-online.org>.
Anderson, Michael (1980), *Approaches to the History of the Western Family 1500-1914*, Macmillan, London.
APworldstream (2002/04), "Swedish Hindus Protest Ikea Advertisement Featuring Toilet Seat Buddha," *Associated Press*. Web. Oct. 2012. <www.highbeam.com>.

Arendt, Hannah (1973), *The Origins of Totalitarianism*, Harvest Books, Fort Washington, PA.
Arendt, Hannah (1993), *Between Past and Future*, Penguin Classics, London.
aTimes (2008/05), "The Young Ones" by William Sparrow, *Asia Times Online*. Web. Oct. 2012. <www.atimes.com>.
aTimes (2008/07), "Midnight in the Kindergarten of Good and Evil," by David P. Goldman, *Asia Times Online*. Web. Oct. 2012. <www.atimes.com>.
Bacon, Francis (1620/2012), *Novum Organum (The New Organon – or True Directions Concerning the Interpretation of Nature)*, Vol.1. Web. Oct. 2012. <www.constitution.org>.
Bapat, Purushottam Vishvanath (1956), *2500 Years of Buddhism*, India Publications Division, Delhi.
Barnett, Thomas (2004), *The Pentagon's New Map: War and Peace in the Twenty-First Century*, G. P. Putnam's Sons, New York.
BBC [British Broadcasting Corporation] (2007/03/27), "Overseas Students 'One in Seven.'" Web. Oct. 2012. <www.bbc.co.uk>.
BBC [British Broadcasting Corporation] (2007/03/29), "Should Apes Have Human Rights?" Web. Oct. 2012. <www.bbc.co.uk>.
BBC [British Broadcasting Corporation] (2008/03/Day?), "Polls Suggest 88% Want EU Vote." Web. Oct. 2012. <www.bbc.co.uk>.
Behler, Ernst et. al (1987), "Nietzsche und das Gesetzbuch des Manu," *Internationales Jahrbuch für die Nietzsche-Forschung*, Vol. 16, Walter de Gruyter, Berlin, pp. 340-352.
Beisner, Robert L. (2006), *Dean Acheson: A Life in the Cold War*, Oxford University Press, Oxford.
Bell, Daniel A. (2000), *East Meets West*, Princeton University Press, Princeton, NJ.
Bell, Daniel A., and Qing Jiang (2012), A Confucian Constitution for China, *The New York Times*, July 10th.

Berger, Peter (1966), *The Social Construction of Reality: A Treatise in the Sociology of Knowledge*, Anchor, Harpswell, ME.

Berger, Peter, and Samuel P. Huntington (1974), *Many Globalizations: Cultural Diversity in the Contemporary World*, Oxford University Press, Oxford.

Berger, Peter (1999), *The Desecularization of the World: Resurgent Religion and World Politics*, Eerdmans, Grand Rapids, MI.

Bernie, Lucie (2005), "Christianity and the Other: Friedrich Schlegel's and F. W. J Schelling's Interpretation of China," *International Journal of Asian Studies*, Vol. 2/2005, pp. 265-273.

Bethel, Dayle M. (1973), *Makiguchi: The Value Creator, Revolutionary Japanese Educator and Founder of Soka Gakkai*, Weatherhill, New York/Tokyo.

Bhagavad Gita (2008), *The Bhagavad Gita in English*. Web. Oct. 2012. <www.bhagavad-gita.org>.

Biagioli, Mario (1999), *The Science Studies Reader*, Routledge, London.

Binford, Lewis, and Kun-ho Chuan (1985), "Taphonomy at a Distance: Zhoukoudian 'The Cave of Peking Man?,'" *Current Anthropology*, Vol. 26, No. 4, pp. 413-442.

Blanchot, Maurice (1983), *Die Uneingestehbare Gemeinschaft*, Suhrkamp, Frankfurt.

Boon, James A. (1972), *From Symbolism to Structuralism: Lévi-Strauss in a Literary Tradition*, Harper & Row, New York.

Borthwick, Mark (1998), *Pacific Century: The Emergence of Modern Pacific Asia*, Westview Press, Boulder, CO.

Boyd, Robert (2003), "The Evolution of Altruistic Punishment," *Proceedings of the National Academy of Sciences of the United States of America*, Vol. 100, No. 6, pp. 3531-3535.

Boyd, Robert, and Peter Richerson (2005), *The Origin and Evolution of Cultures*, Oxford University Press, Oxford.

Brain.web (2007), "Left vs. Right – Which Side Are You On?" Web. Oct. 2012. <www.brain.web-us.com>.

Brannen, Noah S. (1964), "Soka Gakkai's Theory of Value," *Contemporary Religions in Japan*, Vol. 5, No. 2, pp. 146-147.

Breithaupt, Holger (2000), "The Flight from European Science: The Attraction of the American Research System for Young European Scientists," *EMBO Reports*, Vol. 1, No. 2, pp. 104-105.

Butler, Cuthbert (1927), *Western Mysticism*, Constable, London.

Cambridge Dictionary of Philosophy (1999, 2nd ed.), ed. Robert Audi, Cambridge University Press, Cambridge.

Carter, Robert E. (1997), *The Nothingness Beyond Good: An Introduction to the Philosophy of Nishida Kitaro*, 2nd ed., Paragon House, Saint Paul, MN.

Cavalli-Sforza, Luca, Paolo Menozzi, and Alberto Piazza, (1994), *The History and Geography of Human Genes*, Princeton University Press, Princeton, NJ.

CCTV [China Central Television] (2006), Special Documentary: *Daguo Jueqi* (大国崛起, *The Rise of the Great Powers*), Beijing.

China.org (2005), "White Paper on Building of Political Democracy in China," State Council Information Office, Oct. 19, 2005. Web. Oct. 2012. <www.china.org.cn>.

China Daily (2007/10/10), "Baby Boom for the Beijing Olympics," by Addie Chan. Web. Oct. 2012. <www.chinadaily.com.cn>.

China Daily (2008/04/29), "Henan Population Situation." Editorial. Web. Oct. 2012. <www.chinadaily.com.cn>.

China Daily (2012/02/01), "Enter the Dragon Babies," by Cheng Anqi. Web. Oct. 2012. <www.chinadaily.com.cn>.

Chirot, Daniel (1991), Review: "Was Europe Lucky, Evil, or Smart?," *Contemporary Sociology*, Vol. 20, No. 1, pp. 26-28.

Chun, Sue (2004), *Beijing Doll*, Riverhead Trade, New York.

CIA Factbook (2008), *The World Factbook*, Central Intelligence Agency. Web. Oct. 2012. <www.cia.gov>.

Clavell, James (1986), *Shogun* and *Tai-Pan,* Bantam Dell, New York, 2 vols.
CNET (2005), "China's College Population at 19 million," by Michael Kanellos, Aug. 30, 2005. Web. Oct. 2012. <www.cnet.com>.
Confucius [孔子, Kong Zi] (2004), Confucius Texts Online. Web. Feb. 2007. <www.100jia.net>.
Cook, Daniel J., and Henry Rosemont, Jr. (1994), "Discourse on the Natural Theology of the Chinese," *Leibniz: Writings on China*, Open Court, Chicago.
Cooley, Charles H., and Philip Rieff (1983/2003), *Social Organization: A Study of the Larger Mind*, Transaction Publishers, London.
Coolidge, Mary Roberts (1909), *Chinese Immigration*, Arno Press, New York.
Couplet, Philippe (1687), *Confucius Sinarum Philosophus, Sive Scientia Sinensis Latine Exposita*, n.p., Paris.
Daisaku, Ikeda, Xianlin Ji, and Zhongxin Jiang, *Dialogues on Eastern Wisdom*, Sichuan People's Publishing House, Chengdu, P.R. China.
Darwin, Charles (1859/1985), *The Origin of Species*, Penguin, London.
Deary, Ian (2001), *Intelligence: A Very Short Introduction*, Oxford University Press, Oxford.
Deng, Xiaomang (1999), The Union of Chinese and Western Ethics, *Journal for the Study of Christian Culture*, No. 4, pp. 421-423.
Derrida, Jaques (1967), *De la Grammatologie*, Editions de Minuit, Paris.
Destasis (2006), Deutsches Statistisches Bundesamt. Web. Oct. 2012. <www.destasis.de>.
Dewey, John (1929), *The Quest for Certainty: A Study of the Relation of Knowledge and Action*, Minton, Balch and Co., New York.

Diamond, Jared (2003), *Guns, Germs and Steel*, Penguin, London.
Diamond, Jared (2006), *Collapse: How Societies Choose to Fail or Survive*, Penguin, London.
Dong, Zhongshu [董仲舒] (1975), 春秋繁露 (*Luxuriant Dew of the Spring and Autumn Annals*), 四库全书本, Vol. 17, Taiwan Commercial Press, Taipei.
Dunbar, Robin, Chris Knight, and Camilla Power (1999), *The Evolution of Culture*, Edinburgh University Press, Edinburgh.
Durant, William (1930), *The Case for India*, Simon & Schuster, New York.
Duras, Marguerite (1984), *L'Amant* (*The Lover*), Editions Nathan, Paris.
Dw [Deutsche Welle] (2006/02/14), "UN Probes German School Inequality." Web. Oct. 2009. <www.dw-world.de>.
Economist (2006/03/16), "German Demography: Cradle Snatching – The Difficulties of Living with a Low Birth-Rate." Editorial. Web. Oct. 2012. <www.economist.com>.
Economist (2007/02/01), "Tibet: Still Tibetan after All These Years – Economic Advance Is Not Winning All That Many Hearts and Minds." Editorial. Web. Oct. 2012. <www.economist.com>.
Einstein, Albert (1905), " Zur Elektrodynamik Bewegter Körper," *Annalen der Physik*, Vol. 17, pp. 891-921.
Engelfriet, Peter, and Man-Keung Siu (2001), "Xu Guangqi's Attempts to Integrate Western and Chinese Mathematics," *Statecraft and Intellectual Renewal in Late Ming China, The Cross-Cultural Synthesis of Xu Guangqi (1562-1633)*, eds. Catherine Jami, Peter Engelfriet, and Gregory Blue, Brill, Leiden.
Fischer, Steven Roger (2005), *A History of Writing*, Reaktion Books, London.
Flynn, James Robert (1980), *Race, IQ and Jensen*, Routledge and Kegan Paul, London.

Flynn, James Robert (1994), "IQ Gains Over Time," *Encyclopedia of Human Intelligence*, ed. R. J. Sternberg, Macmillan, New York, pp. 617-623.
Foucault, Michel (1977), *Discipline and Punish: The Birth of the Prison*, Allen Lane, London.
Foucault, Michel (1988), *Politics, Philosophy, and Culture: Interviews and Other Writings, 1977-1984*, eds. M. Morris and P. Patton, Routledge, New York.
Fraser, Steven (1995), *The Bell Curve Wars*, Basic Books, New York.
Freytag, Walter (1940/2004), *Spiritual Revolution in the East*, James Clarke and Co., Cambridge.
Friedman, Milton (1962), *Capitalism and Freedom*, Chicago University Press, Chicago.
Friedman, Milton (1990), *Free to Choose*, Harcourt Trade Publishers, New York.
Friedman, Milton (2006), *The Power of Choice*, Free to Choose Media, Erie, PA.
Fülberth, Georg (2007), *Finis Germaniae: Deutsche Geschichte Seit 1945*, Papyrossa Verlagsgesellschaft, Cologne.
Fujiwara, Mashiko (2007), *The Dignity of the Nation*, transl. Murray Giles, IBC Publishing, Tokyo.
Fukuyama, Francis (1992), *The End of History and the Last Man*, Free Press, New York.
Fuller, Gary (1995), "The Demographic Backdrop to Ethnic Conflict: A Geographic Overview," *The Challenge of Ethnic Conflict to National and International Order in the 1990's*, Central Intelligence Agency, Washington, D.C.
Gandhi, Mahatma (1924/1938/2006), *The Collected Works of Mahatma Gandhi*, Vol. 26, Obscure Press, London.
Garrison, Jim (2000), *Civilization and the Transformation of Power*, Paraview Press, New York.
Garth, John (2005), *Tolkien and the Great War: The Threshold of Middle-earth*, Houghton Mifflin, Boston.

Ge, Zhaoguang [葛兆光] (2001),中国思想史 (*The History of Chinese Thought*), Fudan University Press, Shanghai.
Gellert, Claudius (1996), "Recent Trends in German Higher Education," *European Journal of Education*, Vol. 31, No. 3, pp. 311-319.
Gellner, Ernest (1979), *Spectacles and Predicaments: Essays in Social Theory*, Cambridge University Press, Cambridge.
Geohive (2008), GeoHive: Global Statistics, Country Data Pakistan. Web. Oct. 2012. <www.geohive.com>.
Gibney, Alex (1992), "The Pacific Century, New Video and Print Resources for Teaching Asia," *Political Science and Politics*, Vol. 25, No. 2, pp. 237-280.
Goddard, David (1982), Review: "The Age of Structuralism: Lévi-Strauss to Foucault by Edith Kurzweil," *The American Journal of Sociology*, Vol. 87, No. 4, pp. 989-991.
Goethe, Johann Wolfgang von (1790/1999), *Venezianische Epigramme*, Insel Verlag, Frankfurt.
Goethe, Johann Wolfgang von (1833/2006), *Maximen und Reflexionen*, Deutscher Taschenbuch Verlag, München.
Golden, Arthur (1997), *Memoirs of a Geisha*, Vintage Books, London.
Goldman, David P. (2008/05), "The Monster and the Sausage," *Asia Times Online*. Web. Oct. 2012. <www.atimes.com>.
Goldstone, Jack A. (1991), *Revolution and Rebellion in the Early Modern World*, University of California Press, Berkeley, CA.
Gordon, Stewart (2007), *When Asia Was the World*, Da Capo Press, New York.
Gray, Peter B., et al. (2006), "Fathers Have Lower Salivary Testosterone Levels than Unmarried Men and Married Non-Fathers in Beijing, China," *Proceedings of the Royal Society*, *Biological Sciences*, Vol. 273, No. 1584, pp. 333-339.
Gray, Russell D., and Fiona M. Jordan (2000), "Language Trees Support the Express-Train Sequence of Austronesian Expansion," *Nature*, Vol. 405, No. 6790, pp. 1052-1055.

Grieve, Paul (2006), *A Brief Guide to Islam: History, Faith and Politics*, Carroll and Graf, New York.
Griffiths, Bede (1982), *Marriage of East and West: A Sequel to the Golden String*, Templegate Publishers, Springfield, IL.
Gu, Hongming [辜鸿铭] (1922/2005), 中国人的精神 (*The Spirit of the Chinese People*), Guangxi Normal University Publishing House, Guangxi.
Gu, Zhengkun [辜正坤] (1995), *Lao Zi: The Book of Tao and Teh*, Peking University Press, Beijing.
Gu, Zhengkun [辜正坤] (2003), "Value Localization of Chinese and Western Cultures," in 世界文化的东亚视角 *East Asia's View on World Culture*, Peking University Press, Beijing.
Habermas, Jürgen (1996), *The Inclusion of the Other*, MIT Press, Cambridge, MA.
Habermas, Jürgen (2003), *The Future of Human Nature*, Cambridge University Press, Cambridge.
Habermas, Jürgen (2006), *The Divided West*, Cambridge University Press, Cambridge.
Haeckel, Ernst (2004), *The Evolution of Man*, Kessinger Publisher, Whitefish, MT.
Han, Fook Kwang, Warren Fernandez, and Sumiko Tan (1998), *Lee Kuan Yew: The Man and His Ideas*, Times Editions, New York.
Hardt, Michael, and Antonio Negri (2001), *Empire*, Harvard University Press, Cambridge, MA.
Hart, Roger (1999), "On the Problem of Chinese Science," *The Science Studies*, ed. Mario Biagioli, Routledge, London.
Hashimoto, Keizo, and Catherine Jami (2001), "From the Elements to Calender Reform: Xu Guangqi's Shaping of Scientific Knowledge," *Statecraft and Intellectual Renewal in Late Ming China, The Cross-Cultural Synthesis of Xu Guangqi (1562-1633)*, eds. Catherine Jami, Peter Engelfriet, and Gregory Blue, Brill, Leiden.

Haspelmath, Martin et al. (2005), *The World Atlas of Language Structures*, Oxford University Press, Oxford.
Hegel, Georg Wilhelm Friedrich (1821/1956), *The Philosophy of History*, transl. John Sibree, Dover Publications, Mineola, NY.
Heinsohn, Gunnar (2003), *Söhne und Weltmacht – Terror im Aufstieg und Fall der Nationen*, Vols. 1-2, Orell Füssli, Zurich.
Heinsohn, Gunnar (2005), "Finis Germaniae? Reflexionen über Demografische Ursachen von Revolutionen, Kriegen und Politischen Niederlagen," *Die Zeit*-online, Kursbuch 162, Nov. 25, 2005. Web. Oct. 2012. <www.zeit.de >.
Hendry, Joy, and Heung Wah Wong (2006), *Dismantling the East-West Dichotomy: Essays in Honour of Jan van Bremen*, Routledge, NY.
Herrnstein, Richard, and Charles Murray (1994), *The Bell Curve*, Free Press, London.
Hesse, Hermann (1921), "Chinesische Landschaftsmalerei," in *Materialien zu Siddharta*, Suhrkamp, Frankfurt.
Hobbes, Thomas (1651/1989), *Leviathan*, Penguin Classics, London.
Hoe, John (2007), *The Jade Mirror of the Four Unknowns by Zhu Shijie*, Mingming Bookroom Publisher, Christchurch.
Hölldobler, Bert, and Edward Wilson (1990), *The Ants*, Springer, Heidelberg.
Hölldobler, Bert, and Edward Wilson (1994), *Journey to the Ants: A Story of Scientific Exploration*, Belknap/Harvard University Press, Cambridge, MA.
Hofstede, Geert (1991), *Cultures and Organization: Software of the Mind*, McGraw-Hill, New York.
Horng, Wann-Sheng (2001), "The Influence of Euclid's *Elements* on Xu Guangqi and his Successors," *Statecraft and Intellectual Renewal in Late Ming China, The Cross-Cultural Synthesis of Xu Guangqi (1562-1633)*, Brill, Leiden.

Horton, Robin, and Ruth Finnegan (1973), *Modes of Thought: Essays on Thinking in Western and Non-Western Societies*, Faber, London.

Hua, Meng, and Sukehiro Hirakawa (2000), *Images of Westerners in Chinese and Japanese Literature*, Rodopi Press, Amsterdam.

Huang, Chun-chieh (2006), *'Time' and 'Supertime' in Chinese Historical Thinking*, Chinese University Press, Hong Kong.

Human Rights Watch (2003), *Worldreport 2003*. Web. Sept. 2009. <www.hrw.org>.

Huntington, Samuel (1993), *The Clash of Civilizations and the Remaking of World Order*, Touchstone, London.

Huntington, Samuel (2000), *Culture Matters: How Values Shape Human Progress*, Basic Books (Perseus), New York.

Huntington, Samuel (2004), *Who Are We: The Challenge to America's National Identity*, Basic Books (Perseus), New York.

Husserl, Edmund (1935), "The Vienna Lecture," *The Crisis of European Sciences and Transcendental Phenomenology*, Northwestern University Press, Evanston, IL.

Husserl, Edmund (1970), *The Crisis of European Sciences and Transcendental Phenomenology*, Northwestern University Press, Evanston, IL.

Hutcheon, Linda (1989), *The Politics of Postmodernism*, Routledge, London.

Hutton, Will (2007), *The Writing on the Wall: China and the West in the 21st Century*, Little, Brown, London.

Ibn Khaldun (1969), *The Muqaddimah*, trans. Franz Rosenthal, Bollingen, New York.

IIE (2006), "IIE Backgrounder: Educational Exchange with India," *Open Doors*, Nov. 13, 2006. Web. Oct. 2012. <www.opendoors.org>.

Jami, Catherine, Peter Engelfriet, and Gregory Blue (2001), *Statecraft and Intellectual Renewal in Late Ming China, The*

Cross-Cultural Synthesis of Xu Guangqi (1562-1633), Brill, Leiden.

Ji, Xianlin [季羡林] in the foreword of Lin Chengjie [林承节] (1996), 独立后的印度史 (*The History of India after Independence*), 1st ed., Peking University Press, Beijing.

Ji, Xianlin [季羡林] (2006), "Scholars to Create and Carry on Civilizations," *Beijing Forum 2005*, Express-11, May 15, 2006, Xinhua News Agency. Web. Dec. 2006. <www.china.com.cn>.

Ji, Xianlin [季羡林] (2006), 季羡林谈 (*Ji Xianlin Talks*), Contemporary China Publishing House, Beijing.

Ji, Xianlin [季羡林] (2006), 三十年河西，十年河东 (*Thirty Years West of the River, Thirty Years East of It*), Vols.1-6, Contemporary China Publishing House, Beijing.

Jin, Li [金力] et al. (1998), "Hypothetical Ancestral Migration Routes to the Far East," *Proceedings of the National Academy of Sciences of the United States of America*, Sept. 29, Vol. 95, pp. 11763-11768.

Jin, Li [金力] (2006), "Genetic Findings Support 'Out of Africa' Theory," *Texas Medical Center News*, Vol. 20, No. 19. Web. Sept. 2009. <www.tmc.edu>.

Joubert, Joseph (1962), in Wittgenstein, Ludwig: *Lectures and Essays in Criticism (Complete Prose Works of Matthew Arnold)*, Vol.3, University of Michigan Press, Ann Arbor, MI.

Jules, Gary (2006), *Mad World*. Web. Oct. 2012. <www.youtube.com>.

Kakuzo, Okakura (1904/2002), *The Ideals of the East*, Tuttle, North Clarendon, VT.

Kapoor, Kapil (2001), *Decolonizing the Indian Mind, National Seminar on Decolonizing English Education*, Keynote address delivered on Feb. 18, 2001, at the National Seminar on Decolonizing English Education, North Gujarat University, Patan, India. Web. Oct. 2012. <www.ifihhome.tripod.com>.

Kawabata, Yasunari (1969), *The Existence and Discovery of Beauty*, trans. V. H. Viglielmo, The Mainichi Newspapers (Publisher), Tokyo.

Keiji, Nishitani (1942), "My Opinion on the Problem of the Conquest of Modernity," quoted in Fumihiko Sueki (2004), "A New Paradigm for Understanding Japanese Buddhism" presented at the conference Buddhism In (and Out) Place, Oct. 18, 2004, UCLA, Los Angeles.

Kennedy, Paul (1987), *The Rise and Fall of the Great Powers: Economic Change and Military Conflict From 1500 to 2000*, Vintage Books, Colchester, UK.

Khanna, Tarun (2008), *Billions of Entrepreneurs: How China and India Are Reshaping Their Futures – and Yours*, Harvard Business School Press, Cambridge, MA.

Kim, Choong-Ryeol (2006), "Is the 21st Century an Era of the East? – How to Cope with the Major Proposition of the New Century?," Beijing Forum (2006): The Harmony of Civilizations and Prosperity for All – Reflections on the Civilization Modes of Humankind, *Beijing Forum Newsletter*, Vol. 2, No.??, Peking University Press, Beijing.

Kipling, Joseph Rudyard (1999), "The Ballad of East and West," *The Collected Poems*, Indypublish, McLean, VA.

Kluger, Jeffrey (2008), *The Art of Simplexity*, Hyperion, New York.

Krausse, Alexis Sidney (1900), *The Far East, Its History and Its Questions*, G. Richards, London.

Kübler-Ross, Elisabeth (1969), *On Death and Dying*, Routledge, London.

Küng, Hans (1997), *Weltethos für Weltpolitik und Weltwirtschaft*, Piper, Munich.

Küng, Hans (1998), *Reflections on the Universal Declaration of Human Rights: A Fiftieth Anniversary Anthology*, The Netherlands Ministry of Foreign Affairs, Martinus Nijhoff Publishers, The Hague.

Kuhn, Thomas (1970), *The Structure of Scientific Revolutions*, University of Chicago Press, Chicago.

Kumarajiva [鸠摩罗什] (2008), *The Lotus Sutra: Saddharma Pundarika*. Web. Oct. 2012. <www.sacred-texts.com>.

Kuroda, Toshio [黑田候雄] (1990), *Nihon Chusei No Kokka To Shukyo* (*National and Relgious Medieval Japan*), Iwanami Shoten, Tokyo.

Landes, David (2000), "Culture Makes Almost All the Difference," *Culture Matters: How Values Shape Human Progress*, ed.?? , Basic Books (Perseus), New York, pp. 2-14.

Lao Zi [老子] (1876), 道德经 (*The Way of Tao*), trans. James Legge, Trubner, London.

Ledderose, Lothar (2005), "Chinas Zeichenschrift Formt ein Ueberlegenes Denken," *Eurasisches Magazin*, Sept. 30, 2005. Web. Oct. 2012. <www.eurasischesmagazin.de>.

Legge, James (1876), *The Chinese Classics*, Trubner, London.

Leibniz, Gottfried Wilhelm (1994), "Discourse on the Natural Theology of the Chinese," *Writings on China*, trans. Daniel J. Cook and Henry Rosemont, Jr., Open Court, Chicago.

Lenin, Vladimir (1919), "Speech at the Unveiling of a Monument to Stepan Razin on Lobnoye Mesto on May Day," *Lenin's Collected Works*, trans. George Hanna, 4th ed. Vol. 29, Progress Publishers, Moscow.

Lévi-Strauss, Claude (1952), *Race and Culture*, UNESCO, Paris.

Li, Dazhao [李大钊] (2006), quoted in Ji Xianlin [季羡林], 三十年河西，十年河东 (Thirty Years West of the River, Thirty Years East of It), Contemporary China Publishing House, Beijing.

Li, Tiangang [李天刚] (1998), 中国礼仪之争：历史,文献和意义(*The Chinese Rites Controversy: Its History, Documentation and Significance*), Shanghai Classical Publishing House, Shanghai.

Li, Tiangang [李天刚] (2007), *Notes of Explanation for Xu Guangqi, Yang Tingyun, and Li Zhizhao's Christian Writings*, Daofeng Publishing House, Hong Kong.

Li, Wai-Yee (2008), *The Readability of the Past in Early Chinese Historiography*, Harvard East Asian Monographs, Harvard University Press, Cambridge, MA.

Lin, Chengjie [林承节] (1996), 独立后的印度史 (*The History of India after Independence*), 1st ed., Peking University Press, Beijing.

Lin, Justin Yifu (2006), "Opportunities and Challenges in the Research and Education of Economics in China," Beijing Forum (2006): The Harmony of Civilizations and Prosperity for All – Reflections on the Civilization Modes of Humankind, *Beijing Forum Newsletter*, Vol. 2, No. 2, Peking University Press, Beijing.

Lin, Patricia (2007), *Invented Asia: Mimicry and Counter-production in the Arts*, Cal Poly Pomona, CA. Web. Sept. 2009. <http://www.csupomona.edu>.

Liu, E [刘鹗] (c. 1909), 老残游记 (*The Travels of Lao Can*), Foreign Languages Press, Beijing.

Lloyd, Geoffrey Ernest Richard (1996), *Adversaries and Authorities: Investigations into Ancient Greek and Chinese Science*, Cambridge University Press, Cambridge.

Long, John L. (2002), *Madame Butterfly*, Rutgers University Press, Piscataway, NJ.

Loti, Pierre (2001), *Madame Chrysanthème, Oeuvres Complètes de Pierre Loti*, Vol. 4, Adamant Media Corporation, Paris.

Lu, Xun [鲁迅] (1981), 鲁迅全集 (*Collected Works of Lu Xun*), People's Literature Publishing House, Beijing.

Lü, Yaohuai (2005), "Privacy and Data Privacy Issues in Contemporary China," *Ethics and Information Technology*, Vol. 7, No. 1, pp. 7-15.

Luo, Guanzhong [罗贯中] (1998), 三国演义 (*Romance of the Three Kingdoms*), People's Literature Publishing House, Beijing.
Luttwak, Edward Nicolae (1994), "Twilight of the Great Powers: Why We No Longer Will Die for a Cause," *Washington Post*, June 26, 1994, pp. C1-C2.
Luttwak, Edward Nicolae (1995), "Toward Post-Heroic Warfare: The Obsolescence of Total War," *Foreign Affairs*, Vol. 74, No. 3, pp. 109-123.
Lynch, Colum (2007), "Russia, China Veto Resolution on Burma," *The Washington Post*, January 13, 2007, p. A12.
Mace, Ruth, Clare Holden, and Stephen Shennan (2005), *The Evolution of Cultural Diversity: A Phylogentic Approach*, UCL Press, London.
Mackinder, Halford John (1904), "The Geographical Pivot of History," *The Geographical Journal*, Vol. 170, No. 4 (Dec. 2004), pp. 230-321.
Maddison, Angus (2006), "China in the World Economy: 1300-2030," *International Journal of Business*, Vol. 11, No. 3, pp. 239-245.
Maddison, Wayne, Peter Midford, and Sarah Otto (2007), "Estimating a Binary Character's Effect on Speciation and Extinction," *Systematic Biology*, Vol. 56, pp. 701-710.
Mahabharata (2008), ed. John D. Smith, Penguin Classics, London.
Mahbubani, Kishore (1997), *Can Asians Think? Understanding the Divide Between East and West*, Steerforth, Hanover, NH.
Mahbubani, Kishore (2008), *The New Asian Hemisphere: The Irresistible Shift of Global Power to the East*, Public Affairs Publisher, New York.
Malhotra, Rajiv (2011), *Being Different: An Indian Challenge to Western Universalism*, Harper Collins, New Delhi.
Malthus, Thomas (1999), *An Essay on the Principles of Population*, Oxford University Press, Oxford.

Mao, Zedong [毛泽东] (1991), 毛泽东选集 *Mao Zedong: Selected Works*, 人民出版社 People's Publishing House, Beijing.

Mao, Zedong [毛泽东] (1957), 毛泽东同志论《帝国主义和一切反动派都是纸老虎》 (Speech at the Moscow Meeting of Communist and Worker's Parties from Nov. 18, 1957), in 毛泽东选集 (*Mao Zedong: Selected Works*), People's Publishing House, Beijing.

Mao, Zedong [毛泽东] (1960/1964), "新民主主义论" ("On New Democracy"), 毛泽东选集 (*Mao Zedong: Selected Works*), Vol. 2, Foreign Languages Press, Beijing.

Mao, Zedong [毛泽东] (1960), "新民主主义论" ("On New Democracy"), 毛泽东选集 (*Mao Zedong: Selected Works*), Vol. 4, Foreign Languages Press, Beijing.

Mao, Zedong [毛泽东] (1967), *Some Questions Concerning Methods of Leadership*, Foreign Languages Press, Beijing.

Marchand, Suzanne (2001), "German Orientalism and the Decline of the West," *Proceedings of the American Philosophical Society*, Vol. 145, No. 4, pp. 465-473.

Marion, Russ (1999), *The Edge of Organization: Chaos and Complexity – Theories of Formal Social Systems*, Sage Publications, London.

Marr, Wilhelm (1879), *Sieg des Judenthums über das Germanenthum – Vom Nicht Confessionellen Standpunkt aus Betrachtet*, Rudolph Costenoble, Bern.

Marx, Karl (1848), *Manifest der Kommunistischen Partei*, The Communist League, London.

Marx, Karl (1875), *Critique of the Gotha Program*, Progress Publisher, Moscow.

Masuda, Takahiko, and Richard Nisbett (2001), "Attending Holistically Versus Analytically: Comparing the Context Sensitivity of Japanese and Americans," *Journal of*

Personality and Social Psychology, Vol. 81, No. 5, pp. 992-934.
May, Reinhard (1996), *Heidegger's Hidden Sources: East-Asian Influences on His Work*, Routledge, Oxford.
Mazahéri, Aly (1983), *La Route de la Soie*, Papyrus, Paris.
McDougall, Bonnie, and Anders Hansson (2002), *Chinese Concepts of Privacy*, Brill, Leiden.
McGilchrist, Iain (2012), *The Master and His Emissary: The Divided Brain and the Making of the Western World*, Yale University Press, New Haven, CT.
McGregor, James (2007), *One Billion Customers: Lessons from the Front Lines of Doing Business in China*, Free Press Publisher, Glencoe, IL.
Meadows, Donella et al. (1972), *The Limits to Growth*, Chelsea Green Publishing, White River Junction, VT.
Mellman, Ira (2012), 'Chinese Students: A Growing U.S. Business Commodity,' *Voice of America* (VOA), Aug. 7, 2012. Web. <www.voanews.com>.
Mencius [孟子, Meng Zi] (2004), *The Book of Mencius*, Toyo Gakuen University, Department of East Asian Studies, trans. Charles Muller. Web. Oct. 2012. <www.acmuller.net>.
Meng, Hua, and Sukehiro Hirakawa (1997), "Images of Westerners in Chinese and Japanese Literature," *Proceedings of the 15th Congress of the International Comparative Literature Association*, Vol. 10, Rodopi, Amsterdam.
Merton, Robert (1968), *Social Theory and Social Structure*, Free Press, New York.
Miller, Barbara Stoler (1986), *The Bhagavad-Gita: Krishna's Counsel in Time of War*, Columbia University Press, New York.
Minorityinfo (2008), *Der Minority Report: Die Zugelassene Islamisierung Europas*. Web. Oct. 2012. <www.islamisierung.info>.
Monier-Williams, Monier (1894), *Hinduism*, E. & J.B. Young & Co., New York.

Moore, Greg (2003), "From Buddhism to Bolshevism: Some Orientalist Themes in German Thought, German Life and Letters," *German Life and Letters*, Vol. 56, Issue 1, pp. 20-42.

Morgan, Estelle (1958), "Goethe and the Philistine," *The Modern Language Review*, Vol. 53, No. 3, pp. 374-379.

Morita, Akio, and Shintaro Ishihara (1989), *The Japan That Can Say No: Why Japan Will Be First Among Equals*, Simon & Schuster, London.

Murray, Scott (2000), *Liberal Diplomacy and German Unification: The Early Career of Robert Morier*, Praeger, London.

Nakamura, Hajime (1996/2008), *Hindukyo To Jojishi (The Notion of Time in India)*, Shunjusha, Tokyo.

Nandy, Ashis (1989), *Science, Hegemony and Violence: A Requiem for Modernity*, Oxford University Press, Oxford.

Needham, Joseph (1951), *Human Law and the Laws of Nature in China and the West*, Oxford University Press, Oxford.

Needham, Joseph (1954/2000), *Science and Civilization in China*, Cambridge University Press, Cambridge.

Needham, Joseph (1964), "Science and China's Influence on the World," in *The Legacy of China, edited* by Raymond Dawson, Clarendon Press, Oxford.

Needham, Joseph (2004), *The Grand Titration*, Routledge, New York.

Ng, On-cho (1998), Review: "On the 'Logic' of Togetherness – A Cultural Hermeneutic by Kuang-ming Wu," *Philosophy East and West*, Vol. 50, No. 3, The Philosophy of Jainism (July 2000), pp. 461-464.

Nietzsche, Friedrich (1872), *The Birth of Tragedy,* Foulis Press, London.

Nietzsche, Friedrich (1885), *Thus Spoke Zarathustra, Complete Works of Friedrich Nietzsche*, ed. Oscar Levy, Vol. 15, Foulis Press, London.

Nietzsche, Friedrich (1909), *The Will to Power, Complete Works of Friedrich Nietzsche*, ed. Oscar Levy, Vol. 15, Foulis Press, London.
Nietzsche, Friedrich (1909), *Jenseits von Gut und Böse, Complete Works of Friedrich Nietzsche*, ed. Oscar Levy, Vol. 15, Foulis Press, London.
Nilsen, Robert (1988), *South Korea Handbook*, Moon Publications, Chico, CA.
Nisbett, Richard (2004), *The Geography of Thought: How Asians and Westerners Think Differently… and Why*, Free Press, New York.
Nishida, Kitaro (1987), *Last Writings: Nothingness and the Religious World View*, trans. David Dillworth, University of Hawaii Press, Honolulu.
Nishida, Kitaro (1989), *Nishida Kitaro Zenshu (Complete Works of Nishida Kitaro in Nineteen Volumes)*, 4th ed., Iwanami Shoten, Tokyo.
Nishida, Kitaro (1990), *An Inquiry into the Good*, trans. Masao Abe and Christopher Ives, Yale University Press, New Haven, CT.
Nishida, Kitaro (2006), *Complete Works of Nishida Kitaro*, transl. by A. Takeda and K. Riesenhueber, Vol. 14, Iwanami Shoten, Tokyo.
Noël, François (1711), *Sinensis imperii libri classici sex*, Societatis Jesu Missionario, Prague.
Nolde, John J. (1966), *A Plea for a Regional Approach to Chinese History: The Case of the South China Coast*, The University of Hong Kong Libraries, Hong Kong. Web. Oct. 2012. <www.lib.hku.hk>.
Orleans, Leo A. (1988), *Chinese Students in America: Policies, Issues, and Numbers*, National Academy Press, Washington, D.C.
Otto, Rudolf (1924), *The Idea of the Holy*, Oxford University Press, London.
Otto, Rudolf (1926), *Mysticism East and West*, Oxford University Press, London.

Pan, Suiming (2004), "Three 'Red Light Districts' in China," *Sexual Cultures in East Asia: The Social Construction of Sexuality and Sexual Risk in a Time of AIDS*, ed. Evelyne Micollier, Routledge Curzon, New York, pp. 25-53.
Paris, John (1947), *Kimono*, Penguin Classics, London.
PBS [Public Broadcasting Service] (1993), *The Pacific Century*, TV documentary written by Alex Gibney, Release date: 1992; aired on PBS in 1993.
Pelliot, Paul, and Arthur Christopher Moule (1938), "Marco Polo – The Description of the World," *The Journal of the Royal Asiatic Society*, Vol. 71, Issue 4, pp. 628-644.
People's Daily (2006/04/05), "Students Again Make Beeline to U.S. Colleges," by Wang Shanshan. Web. Oct. 2012. <www.peopledaily.com.cn>.
Perrett, Roy (1999), "History, Time, and Knowledge in Ancient India," *History and Theory*, Vol. 38, No. 3, pp. 307-321.
Peyrefitte, Alain (1989), *L'Empire Immobile ou le Choc des Mondes*, Fayard, Paris.
Peyrefitte, Alain (1993), *The Collision of Two Civilizations: The British Expedition to China in 1792-4*, Harvill, London.
Phelps, Edmund S. (2007), "Entrepreneurial Culture: Why European Economies Lag Behind the U.S.," *The Wall Street Journal*, Feb. 12, 2007. Web. Oct. 2012. <www.wsj.com>.
Planck, Max (1901), "On the Law of Distribution of Energy in the Normal Spectrum," *Annalen der Physik*, Vol. 4, No.??, pp. 553-559.
Plekhanov, Valentinovich Georgy (1891), *The Materialist Conception of History*. Web. Oct. 2012. <www.marxists.org>.
Polo, Marco (2007), *The Travels*, Cosimo Books, New York.
Pye, Lucian W. (2000), "Asian Values: From Dynamos to Dominos?" *Culture Matters: How Values Shape Human Progress*, edited by Lawrence E. Harrison and Samuel P. Huntington, Basic Books (Perseus), New York, pp. 244-256.

Pyle, Kenneth (2007), *Japan Rising: The Resurgence of Japanese Power and Purpose*, Public Affairs Books, New York.

Qian, Binsi [钱宾四] (1990/1998), 中华思想史(*History of Chinese Thought*), 钱宾四先生全集 (*The Complete Works of Mr. Qian Binsi*), edited by Mu Qian, Lianjing Publishing House, Beijing.

Radhakrishnan, S. (1929/1974), *Hinduism*, quoted in Saral Jhingran (1989), *Aspects of Hindu Morality*, Motilal Banarsidass Publisher, Delhi.

Ramesh, Jairam (2002), *Kautilya Today: Compendium of Essays Between 1998 and 2002*, India Research Press, New Delhi.

Reid, Thomas Roy (2004), *The United States of Europe: The New Superpower and the End of American Supremacy*, Penguin Press, London.

Reynolds, Vernon, and Ralph Tanner (1983), *The Biology of Religion*, Longman, London.

Richardson, Robert D., Jr. (1988), *Henry Thoreau: A Life of the Mind*, University of California Press, Berkeley, CA.

Roberts, Paul (2004), *The End of Oil: On the Edge of a Perilous New World*, Houghton Mifflin, New York.

Rosan, Laurence J. (1962), "Are Comparisons between the East and the West Fruitful for Comparative Philosophy?," *Philosophy East and West*, Vol. 11, No. 4, pp. 239-243.

Rosenthal, Franz (1969), *Ibn Khaldun: The Muqaddimah*, Bollingen, New York.

Rousseau, Jean-Jacques (1672/2007), *The Social Contract, or Principles of Political Right*, transl. George D. H. Cole. Web. Oct. 2012. <www.constitution.org>.

Rushton, Jean Philippe, and Arthur Robert Jensen (2006), "Thirty Years of Research on Race Differences in Cognitive Ability," in *Psychology, Public Policy, and Law*, Vol. 11, No. 2, pp. 235-294.

Russell, Bertrand (1922/1993), *The Problem of China*, Spokesman Books, Nottingham, UK.

Russell, Bertrand (1953), *Mysticism and Logic*, Penguin Books, Harmondsworth /London.
Said, Edward W. (1995), *Orientalism*, Penguin Books, London.
Sapir, Edward (1983), *Selected Writings of Edward Sapir in Language, Culture, and Personality*, ed. David G. Mandelbaum, University of California Press, Berkeley, CA.
Schelling, Friedrich (1842), *Philosophie der Mythologie*. Web. Oct. 2012. <www.phillwebb.net>.
Schopenhauer, Arthur (1819), *Die Welt als Wille und Vorstellung*, Vol. 2, Diogenes, Zurich.
Schröder, Gerhard (2008), "Warum Wir Peking Brauchen," *Die Zeit*, July 17, 2008. Web. Oct. 2012. <www.zeit.de>.
Sen, Amartya Kumar (2006), "Our Global Civilization," Keynote Speech at the Beijing Forum (2006): The Harmony of Civilizations and Prosperity for All – Reflections on the Civilization Modes of Humankind, *Beijing Forum Newsletter,* Vol. 2, No. 2, Peking University Press, Beijing.
Sen, Amartya Kumar (2007), *Identity and Violence: The Illusion of Destiny (Issues of Our Time)*, W. W. Norton, New York.
Shenkar, Oded (2004), *The Chinese Century: The Rising Chinese Economy and Its Impact on the Global Economy, the Balance of Power, and Your Job*, Wharton School Publishing, Philadelphia.
Shibusawa, Naoko (2006), *America's Geisha Ally: Re-imagining The Japanese Enemy*, Harvard University Press, Cambridge, MA.
Shiel, Matthew Phipps (1898), *The Yellow Danger*, Routledge, Oxford.
Shippey, Tom (2002), *J. R. R. Tolkien: Author of the Century*, Houghton Mifflin, Boston.
Siow, Maria (2012), "U.S. Launches Initiative to Boost Number of American Students in China," *Asia Pacific News*, July 9, 2012. Web. Oct. 2012. <www.channelnewsasia.com>.

Sisci, Francesco (2008), "A New World under One Heaven," *Asia Times*, July 4, 2008. Web. Oct. 2012. <www.atimes.com>.
Smith, Arthur Henderson (1890/2003), *Chinese Characteristics*, Ross & Perry Publishing, Haddonfield, NJ.
Smith, Brian (2008), "Time – India – Bibliography," *Science Encyclopaedia: The History of Ideas*, Vol. 6. Web. Oct. 2012. <www.science.jrank.org>.
Song, Qiang [宋强] et al. (1996), 中国可以说不 (*China Can Say No*), China Industry & Commerce Associated Press, Beijing.
Spence, Jonathan D. (2001), *The Search for Modern China*, W.W. Norton, New York.
Spencer, Herbert (1857), "Progress: Its Law and Causes," *The Westminster Review*, Vol. 67, April 1857, pp. 445-465.
Spencer, Herbert (1893), *The Principles of Ethics*, Williams & Norgate, London.
Spengler, Oswald (1917/1922), *The Decline of the West*, Alfred A. Knopf, New York.
Spiegel magazine (2008/07/15), "Olympische Spiele: Altkanzler Schröder Nimmt an Eröffnungsfeier Teil." Editorial. Web. Oct. 2012. <www.spiegel.de>.
Stambaugh, Joan (1999), *The Formless Self*, State University of New York Press, New York.
Sternberg, Robert (1994), *Encyclopedia of Human Intelligence*, Macmillan, New York.
Sueki, Fumihiko (2004), "A New Paradigm for Understanding Japanese Buddhism," presented at the conference Buddhism In (and Out) Place, Oct. 18, 2004, UCLA, Los Angeles.
Suzuki, Daisetsu Teitaro (1994), *An Introduction to Zen Buddhism,* Grove Press, New York.
Tacitus, Publius Cornelius (1996), *Germania*, trans. J.B. Rives, Oxford University Press, Oxford.
Tagore, Rabindranath (1931), *The Religion of Man*, Allen & Unwin, London.

Taylor, McComas (2008), "Six Easy Lessons in Sanskrit," *The Australian National University News*, Summer 2007. Web. Oct. 2012. <www.anu.edu.au>.

Taz (2008/02/12), "Dänische Mohammed-Karikaturen-Zeichner Sollte Getötet Werden," by Reinhard Wolff. Web. Oct. 2012. <www.taz.de>.

Temple, Robert, and Joseph Needham (2007), *The Genius of China: 3,000 Years of Science, Discovery, and Invention*, Inner Traditions International Ltd., Rochester, VT.

TimeEurope (2004), "How to Plug Europe's Brain Drain," by Jeff Chu, Jan. 11, 2004. Web. Oct. 2012. <www.time.com>.

Times (2008), "A Third of Muslim Students Back Killings," by Abul Taher, July 27, 2008. Web. Oct. 2012. <www.thetimes.co.uk>.

Tipitaka, Abhidharmmapitaka (2008), *The Pali Tipitaka Online*. Web. Oct. 2012. <www.tipitaka.org>.

Toynbee, Arnold Joseph, and D.C. Somervell (1958), *Civilization on Trial and the World and the West*, Meridian Books, New York.

Toynbee, Arnold Joseph, and Daisaku Ikeda (1976), *The Toynbee-Ikeda Dialogue: Man Himself Must Choose*, Kodansha International, New York.

Tu, Weiming (2000), "Multiple Modernities: A Preliminary Inquiry into the Implications of East Asian Modernity," *Culture Matters: How Values Shape Human Progress*, edited by Lawrence E. Harrison and Samuel P. Huntington, Basic Books (Perseus), New York, pp. 256-268.

Tu, Weiming (2003), *Dialogue among Civilizations: The Message of China's Rise to the World*, Social Sciences Document Publication House, Beijing.

Tu, Weiming (2012), "Proposal for Establishing the World Ethics Institute at Peking University," The Institute for Advanced Humanistic Studies, Peking University, Beijing.

Tuathail, Georoid O., Simon Dalby, and Paul Routledge, eds. (2006), *The Geopolitics Reader*, Routledge, New York.

Twain, Mark (1897/1989), *Following the Equator: A Journey around the World*, Dover Publications, Mineola, NY.

U Ko Lay, Sayagyi (1990), *Guide to Tipitaka*, Sri Satguru Publications, Delhi.

United Nations (2001), "Year of Dialogue among Civilization," United Nations Department of Public Information. Web. Oct. 2012. <www.un.org>.

United Nations Population Division (2004/2007), *World Population Prospects: The 2004 Revision, Analytical Report*, Vol. 3, United Nations Department of Economic and Social Affairs. Web. Oct. 2012. <www.un.org>.

United Nations Population Division (2006), *Challenges of World Population in the 21st Century: The Changing Age Structure of Population and Its Consequences for Development*, United Nations Department of Economic and Social Affairs. Web. Oct. 2012. <www.un.org>.

Wallerstein, Immanuel (2005), *The U.S., India, and China*, Commentary No. 166, Aug. 1, 2005, Binghamton University. Web. Oct. 2012. <www.binghamton.edu>.

Wall Street Journal (2006/11/11), "Is Admissions Bar Higher for Asians at Elite Schools?" by Daniel Golden. Web. Oct. 2012. <www.wsj.com>.

Wang, Youxuan (2001), *Buddhism and Deconstruction – Towards a Comparative Semiotics*, Curzon Press, Surrey, UK.

Weber, Max (2001), *The Protestant Ethic and the Spirit of Capitalism*, trans. Talcott Parsons, Routledge, New York.

Wei, Hui (2002), *Shanghai Baby*, Washington Square Press, New York.

Wei, Yuan [魏源] (1843), 海国图志 (*Illustrated Records of Overseas Countries*), Zhongzhou Guji Publishing House, Suzhou, P.R. China.

Werber, Bernard (1991), *Empire of the Ants*, Bantam, New York.

Wieger, Léon (1965), *Chinese Characters: Their Origin, Etymology, History, Classification and Signification*, Parragon Books, New York.

Wikipedia (2008), "Dichotomy." Web. Aug. 2008. <www.wikipedia.org>.

Wikipedia (2008), "Völker Europas, Wahrt Eure Heiligsten Güter (People of Europe, Safeguard Your Most Valuable Goods)." Web. Aug. 2008. <www.wikipedia.org>.

Wikipedia (2008), "World's most best-selling books." Web. Aug. 2008. <www.wikipedia.org>.

Williams, Paul, Kate Crosby, and Andrew Skilton, eds. (1998), *The Bodhicaryavatara*, Oxford University Press, Oxford.

Williamson, W. (1977), "Patterns of Educational Inequality in West Germany," *Comparative Education*, Vol. 1, No. 1, pp. 29-44.

Wittgenstein, Ludwig, Matthew Arnold, and R.H. Super, (1962), *Lectures and Essays in Criticism,* Vol. 3, University of Michigan Press, Ann Arbor, MI.

Wu, Kuangming [吴光明] (1997), *On Metaphoring: A Cultural Hermeneutic*, Brill, Leiden.

Wu, Kuangming [吴光明] (1998), *On the "Logic" of Togetherness: A Cultural Hermeneutic*, Brill, Leiden.

Wu, Kuangming [吴光明] (2007), Review: "Notions of Time in Chinese Historical Thinking by Chun-Chieh Huang and John R. Henderson," *Taiwan of East Asian Studies*, Vol. 4, No. 1 (Issue 7), pp. 179-183.

Wu, Kuangming [吴光明] (2008), *China-West Interculture: Toward the Philosophy of World Integration – Essays on Wu Kuang-Ming's Thinking*, ed. Jay Goulding, Global Scholarly Publisher, New York.

Wu, Wenjun [吴文俊] (2007), "An Essay Written on the Occasion of the 400th Anniversary of the Publication of Xu Guangqi's Translation of Euclid's *Elements of Geometry*." Web. Oct. 2012. <www.picb.ac.cn/xuguangqi>.

Xia, Y. R., and Z. G. Zhou (2003), "The Transition of Courtship, Mate Selection and Marriage in China," *Mate Selection across Cultures*, eds. R. R. Hamon et al., Sage Publications, Thousand Oaks, CA, pp. 231-246.

Yang, Zhenning [杨振宁] (2004), 《易经》对中华文化的影响 (The *I Ching*'s Influence on the Development of Modern Science in China), Culture Summit Forum Beijing, The Chinese Culture Promotion Society, Beijing. Web. Oct. 2012. <http://www.people.com.cn>.

Yuan, Xingpei [袁行霈] et al. (2006), 中华文明史 (*A History of the Chinese Civilization*), Peking University Press, Beijing.

Zaehner, Robert Charles (1976), *Concordant Discord*, Oxford University Press, Oxford.

Zhao, Tingyang [赵厅阳] (2005), 天下体系 (*The System of All under Heaven*), Jiangsu Educational Publisher, Jiangsu.

Zhou, Xiaoyi (2000), "Oscar Wilde: An Image of Artistic Self-Fashioning in Modern China: 1909-1949," *Images of Westerners in Chinese and Japanese Literature*, ed. Hua Meng, Rodopi Press, Amsterdam, pp. 95-113.

Zinn, Howard (1980), *A People's History of the United States, 1492 – Present*, HarperCollins, New York.

Zizek, Slavoj (2001), *On Belief*, Routledge, New York.

www.ingramcontent.com/pod-product-compliance
Ingram Content Group UK Ltd.
Pitfield, Milton Keynes, MK11 3LW, UK
UKHW021314180426
11947UKWH00015B/1217